THE CHEAPSKATE'S GUIDE TO
THEME PARKS

THE CHEAPSKATE'S GUIDE TO
THEME PARKS

STEVEN J. URBANOWICZ

CITADEL PRESS
Kensington Publishing Corp.
www.kensingtonbooks.com

CITADEL PRESS BOOKS are published by

Kensington Publishing Corp.
850 Third Avenue
New York, NY 10022

All Kensington titles, imprints, and distributed lines are available at special quantity discounts for bulk purchases for sales promotions, premiums, fund-raising, educational, or institutional use. Special book excerpts or customized printings can also be created to fit specific needs. For details, write or phone the office of the Kensington special sales manager: Kensington Publishing Corp., 850 Third Avenue, New York, NY 10022, attn: Special Sales Department, phone 1-800-221-2647.

CITADEL PRESS and the Citadel logo are Reg. U.S. Pat. & TM Off.

First printing: March 2004

10 9 8 7 6 5 4 3 2 1

Printed in the United States of America

Library of Congress Control Number: 2003109451

ISBN 0-8065-2365-4

for Roxan

Acknowledgments

I thank my mom, Carolyn, and my family for their support.

To Roxan, thank you for being there for the last twenty years!

Special thanks to Kristin Seibeneicher, Gail Rios, and Pat Klingensmith for all their help and friendship throughout the years, and also to Janice Witherow for exactly the same thing.

Special nod to Robert Camuto for support, as well as being my oldest, *oooldest* friend in the world of parks and roller coasters, and to Bill Galvin for his input.

And to Mick Foley, wrestling and roller coaster-riding-superstar, it was a pleasure conquering Nitro with you!

The author (right) enjoys a calm moment with Gill Rios, Vinnie Mazella, and Gail Rios at Six Flags Great Adventure. *(Author's collection)*

Contents

THE CHEAPSKATE'S GUIDE TO
THEME PARKS

1

GETTING STARTED
The Basics for Smart Theme Park Guests

PLANNING TO GO

When visiting a theme park, the last thing you want are crowds, which, in the long run, will be the biggest thing preventing you from making the most of your day. Most people don't realize it, but there are ways to avoid them, and these methods are not as complicated as you'd think. It just takes a bit of planning to have the park relatively to yourself.

The best way to avoid mob scenes is to choose a day when the weather isn't exactly at its best. You're not paying admission to the property to sit on a bench and enhance your tan; you're looking for excitement and entertainment, and you don't need a warm, sunny day for that. Rain, or the threat of it, keeps park crowds down quite considerably, and it definitely deters people from going on rides. (The same people who will wait two hours to get soaked on a river rapids ride won't even think about going on a roller coaster in the rain—they might get a bit wet! Go figure.) If the weather forecast is calling for a chance of thunderstorms, even better. A twenty-minute thunder-and-lightning show will empty a park out like a skunk in a cave. The weather ploy can backfire, however, if the park you're planning to visit doesn't run its rides in the rain. Most do, unless there is lightning, but some actually shut down their rides at the first sign of a drizzle. You might think you're avoiding the crowds, and you will be, but the rides you want to go on might not be available. Call the park before your visit, and ask them if they run rides such as roller coasters in rain. If the answer is yes, the park is yours.

If you know when you're going to be visiting the park well in advance, call and ask if there are any large groups scheduled to visit the same day as you. Sometimes corporate or school groups numbering in the thousands are booked into the parks, and you'll want to know about them, since the only time they won't be running rampant throughout the park is during lunchtime. Don't be surprised, however, if the park refuses to give you this information, since they are not obligated to discourage people from visiting, even when they know the park will provide a less-than-stellar visit to the daytripper. If you don't get the info you need, call back in a day or two and ask for the Group Sales Department, pretending to be a representative of a large group seeking to make a reservation for the day you want to visit. Ask if you will be sharing the day with other large groups. They'll tell you the info you need and suggest an alternative if that day is particularly crowded. You can tell them you'll call them back after you've consulted with your co-workers/board-of-directors/whoever you need to "consult" with. Just be sure you make up a fake company name, and whatever you do, don't give them your real phone number if they ask for one.

ADMISSION

The big theme parks these days average about $40 for a single, one-day admission. Now, considering that you will most likely be spending over twelve hours in the park, that's still a better price than say, a ticket to a concert or sporting event. However, you don't want to give the park a full-price admission. Trust me, they don't care if you do, either, since admissions do not make up the bulk of the profits for a park (in-park spending does). Call the park before your visit and ask them point blank where you can get discount tickets or coupons. Most parks offer some sort of tie-in at fast food chains, supermarkets, and even convenience stores. Certain food products offer coupons. You can often find discount admissions as part of hotel packages that are located near the park as well. The park will be happy to tell you where they have placed these discounts, as they are involved in a cross-promotion with the other company that both find mutually beneficial. Never pay full price to visit a park. Only the "little" people do that.

I've found that if you complain about your day with vim and vigor to Guest Services, they will at the very least offer a comp ticket for a return (I didn't pay admission to one park for three years with this method). If you really feel the need, complain about something. Demand to be satisfied. Don't take no for an answer.

One more little tip: On the outside chance that you only want to run into a park and go on one ride (perhaps the big new roller coaster for that season), call ahead and ask if the park offers a shopping pass. You leave the price of admission at Guest Services as a deposit, are permitted to be in the park for either thirty or sixty minutes to "shop", and if you return back to Guest Services within the hour, you get your money back. If you really feel the need to do this, pick a very rainy day that you know the park will be empty, run in and hop on the ride, and make sure you are back at the front gate within the allotted time.

Parking tolls have risen to amounts as high as $10 for non-priority spaces. Yes, there are ways around paying the parking tolls, but you'll have to figure them out for yourself, since some of them are somewhat less than ethical (in the specific park chapters, there are a few special hints given pertaining to each particular park, however). One very legitimate way to get into the parking lot at a substantial discount is if you own a season pass to the park, and purchase a season parking pass, which will permit you season-long parking for the price of two visits.

Season Passes

If you plan on visiting a park more than once in a season, or think you might be travelling, definitely consider a season pass. For the price of about two visits, a season pass will obtain unlimited admission to the park where you purchase it. Even better, most park chains will allow you to use a season pass purchased at one of its parks at any other park within the chain.

Use the guide below to determine if a season pass purchase is in your future. All parks listed in each grouping are accessible with a season pass purchased at any one of them.

CEDAR FAIR, LP

Cedar Point, Sandusky, Ohio

ValleyFair, Shakopee, Minnesota

Dorney Park and Wildwater Kingdom, Allentown, Pennsylvania

Worlds of Fun and Oceans of Fun, Kansas City, Missouri

Knott's Berry Farm, Buena Park, California

Michigan's Adventure, Muskegon, Michigan

PARAMOUNT PARKS

Paramount's Kings Island, Cincinnati, Ohio

Paramount's Kings Dominion, Doswell, Virginia

Paramount's Great America, Santa Clara, California

Paramount's Carowinds, Charlotte, South Carolina

Paramount Canada's Wonderland, Toronto, Ontario

SIX FLAGS THEME PARKS

Six Flags Over Texas, Arlington, Texas

Six Flags Over Georgia, Atlanta, Georgia

Six Flags St. Louis, Allenton, Missouri

Six Flags Astroworld, Houston, Texas

Six Flags Great Adventure, Jackson, New Jersey

Six Flags Magic Mountain, Valencia, California

Six Flags Great America, Gurnee, Illinois

Six Flags Fiesta Texas, San Antonio
Six Flags Kentucky Kingdom, Louisville, Kentucky
Six Flags America, Largo, Maryland
Six Flags Darien Lake, Corfu, New York
Six Flags Elitch Gardens, Denver, Colorado
Six Flags New England, Agawam, Massachusetts
Six Flags Worlds of Adventure, Aurora, Ohio
Six Flags Marine World, Vallejo, California
Six Flags New Orleans, Louisiana

(Certain park season passes also include admission to additional parks in the Six Flags family. Check when you make your purchase.)

Season passes at all chains must be processed at the park you bought it before admission to other parks in the chain is permitted. This means that you may have bought the pass at a park that opens a month later than another one nearby—you'll just have to take into consideration that you're getting something for free, and therefore shouldn't complain.

RIDES

On average, park guests will go on about eight or nine rides all day (and it will take that long to get on them, with waiting in line). Parks are now offering fast-lane services, whereby you wait one time and get passes to the rides of your choice which have a time stamped on them, and you simply show up at the ride at the designated time and board immediately. However, certain parks are up-charging for this feature, and if that's the case, by no means do you want to fork over even more money than you already have, since what you're paying for is nothing more than a "legal" way to cut the line. The rub is that on roller coasters, for example, the seat you'll be assigned is always the least popular one. If you don't care about that sort of thing, and the service is free, go right ahead and sign up. If you want the front seat, though, you're not getting it through any short cuts, so a fast-pass won't really give you what you want. One general recommendation for avoiding long lines, other than going to the park on a rainy day, is to save any type of "family" oriented attraction for late evening, as the types who will usually choose those rides leave parks earlier. Another good general rule is to enter the park when it opens and immediately head to the major rides that are farthest away from the entrance, as they won't have lines 'til a bit later in the day, and hit those late at night, since the crowds will be heading back to the exit of the park. Each park has different crowd traffic patterns though, so this will only work at certain parks.

Water rides are extremely popular at theme parks, especially on hot days. Lines can build up to two hours or more for any type of water-based attraction, particularly at midday when the sun is at its strongest. Avoid them at this time, and instead ride early in the morning, or after dinner. Yes, the more practical side is to ride these devices when it's hotter than hell and you need to cool off, but waiting in a long line in the heat will actually make you even more uncomfortable. If you look at it from the point of view of going on the ride to enjoy the ride, rather than for the sole purpose of cooling off, you'll enjoy it more, and use up less time. Many theme park water rides, such as flumes, tend to not get you as soaked as you'd like anyway. Choose to do those later, even after dark, and you won't get so wet that you'll be uncomfortable. Rapids and chutes rides, which do tend to get you sopping, are best done in the morning. If all you want to do is cool off, look for one of the many "misters" most parks have set up throughout the property, where you can simply stand under a cool, light spray of water for a few seconds without ever having to stand on any lines.

The philosophy in theme parks is to have major one-of-a-kind attractions throughout the park, with the spinning type rides found at carnivals spread throughout as filler. Theme parks never operate these types of rides at maximum speed, and they also give quite short ride cycles on them. Therefore, it is not worth waiting for any type of spinning ride at a major theme park, unless it is either unique, operated in a manner that is different from any place else that has that particular type of ride, or it has absolutely no line at all. For the most part, you can find these rides just about everywhere, and there is no reason you should waste time riding any of them when major, unique attractions await.

SHOWS

For the most part, shows are free at all parks. If you want to see the best version of any show, see the second show of the day. The first might not have the entire cast on stage, and subsequent ones will have cast members missing because of dinner breaks. I've found the second show of the day to have the entire cast, already warmed up, and performing at full throttle. Surprisingly, while entire casts may offer varying levels of talent, many of the performers are Broadway quality, so you might actually be seeing a future superstar.

GAMES

Play one or two games, if you really need to. Otherwise, avoid them. They are expensive, offer prizes that you could buy for far, far less money (you might spend $10 on something that cost the park eight cents), and you really don't need that giant stuffed animal anyway, right? If it's the kids who are begging to win a prize, look for games near kiddie lands that are less expensive than the regular adult games, most of which have an "Every player wins a prize" policy. As a rule, though, remember that the games are designed to score a win for the park, not the guest.

EATING

On very rare occasions, park food can be quite good. Unfortunately, the rest of the time, it's lukewarm slop you wouldn't feed to your mother-in-law. If you really need that cold rubber hot dog, plan on only one meal for the day. A better suggestion, though, is to get to the park about an hour and a half earlier than the gates open. The roads to almost every theme park in the country are chock-filled with restaurants, ranging from fast food to diners to what-have-you. Grab breakfast there, and make it a light one. For lunch, bring a cooler and either eat in the picnic area the park provides or have a tail-gate party at your car in the parking lot. You can usually even find delis on the road to the park where you can get a bountiful picnic lunch at about one quarter the cost of what the inedible stuff will cost you inside the park. If you think it's going to save you time to eat at a restaurant in the park, think again. Lines in restaurants during peak hours of lunch and dinner can consume more time than it would take to go to the car and grab the hero sandwich out of the cooler. And even though the "No food may be brought into the park" rule is strictly enforced, if you claim to have special dietary needs for either health or religious reasons, you will be permitted to bring just about anything you want to eat in through the gates with you.

SHOPPING

On very rare occasions, a decent t-shirt can be found in a park for about $12. The norm, though is to pay about $20, and let's face it, you're not going to wear these items to a cotillion. Check on the park map, or with Guest Services, and ask if there is a "cheap" discount merchandise shop. Many parks put last year's merchandise in one shop, and offer considerable discounts on all of it. (I managed to find a $35 embroidered collared polo shirt for $1.98 once.) I know it's difficult to pass up certain items though, and there may be discounts offered through season passes or the use of certain credit cards. Always ask, don't impulse buy. I've also found that sometimes, information gets crossed, and the same item in one shop is a lower price than in another. Check around.

ARRIVAL AND DEPARTURE

No matter how much you've spent for the day at the park, you'll want to get as much bang for the buck as you can. The only way to do this is to arrive at the park at least one half-hour earlier than the posted opening time, so you'll be among the first guests to be let inside the gates. You'll get to do things in the park before the main crowds get there.

At the end of the day, the question is whether to leave early to beat the traffic congestion that will undoubtedly pile up at the parking lot exits, or to stay 'til the bitter end. One simple piece of information needs to be asked of Guest Services: "What time are the lines to the rides closed?" Most parks will allow you to get in line right up 'til the posted closing time of the park, while others cut the line much earlier so that the actual rides can close at the posted closing time. You need to find out what the policy is for the park you're visiting. If the park closes all ride lines exactly at the posted *park* closing time, then you should save a big ride that has had a long line all day 'til within a few minutes of closing. You'll actually have spent the time on line waiting after the park is technically "closed," and not during the day when you could have been doing other things. Also, unless you leave a park hours earlier than closing time, you're gonna sit in traffic no matter what you do. Wouldn't you rather be waving from a roller coaster than sitting in traffic? And by doing this, you'll also have bought yourself additional time in the park. Whether you've spent $10 or $50, additional free time is a good and welcome thing.

2

VARIOUS PARK POLICIES YOU NEED TO KNOW

All parks have the same basic general polices, rules, and services. Some of them are as follows:

Alcoholic beverages are not permitted anywhere on park property.

Cameras are not allowed on rides.

Proper dress is required, with shirts and shoes worn at all times, and no profane or offensive words on clothing.

Food may not be brought into parks.

Smoking is not permitted in kiddie areas, any queue lines, all enclosed buildings, restrooms, and theaters.

Line jumping, or saving a place in line for others, is prohibited.

Unruly behavior—profanity, running through the park, etc.—is frowned upon.

Hand-stamps are necessary if you leave the park and plan to return the same day.

Handicapped policies: Most parks offer special services for physically challenged guests. Most amusement rides are generally wheelchair accessible and are available to most guests, depending on what the individual's disability may be. Most parks have a booklet that describes each ride's requirements, which is available at Guest Services. This booklet can be mailed to you in advance of your visit.

Parent swap policies exist at most parks. When height restrictions prohibit a younger child from riding a ride, most parks offer a "parent swap" program for couples and families who wish to ride but do not have non-riding adults to leave the children with. One adult rides the ride while the other waits at the exit of the ride with the kids. When the first adult has ridden, he or she switches places with the one who first stayed with the little ones, affording both adults a ride without waiting in line two separate times. Parks do not typically advertise this policy, and the logistics may vary from park to park, so check with Guest Services regarding the exact policy in effect at the park before you attempt to ride in this manner.

Riding rules are in place for a reason. While you might be at a park for a day of fun and frolic, don't forget that rides are *big pieces of machinery*, and it's important to follow the park's rules to ride for each. Therefore, don't stand up during the ride, allow the restraints to do their job, stay in the seat you started out in, etc. Using a little common sense will prevent you from becoming a headline in tomorrow's newspaper.

3

THE "BESTS" LISTS

These are the "Don't Miss" rides and attractions culled from the parks covered in this book.

TOP FIVE WOOD COASTERS

1. PHOENIX—Knoebels Amusement Resort, Elysburg, Pennsylvania

   This 1948 classic was moved from its defunct home park in Texas to a new location in Pennsylvania in 1985. It has a figure-8 configuration, and features amazing airtime on nearly every hill. The ride has a beautiful setting, is extremely well-maintained, and when it's running well (which is just about all the time), it's just about the best wooden roller coaster experience in the world. This is the *perfect*, quintessential coaster with nothing up its sleeve but pure, unadulterated, and, most importantly, *fun* thrills.

2. TWISTER—Knoebels Amusement Resort, Elysburg, Pennsylvania

   This recreation of a fabled, defunct coaster in Denver, Colorado actually improves on the original design in many ways. The perfectly shaped first few drops lead to the intense double helix that the coaster is named for, and the overall design offers

The amazingly perfect Phoenix at Knoebels Amusement Resort. *(Bill Galvin)*

hidden drops, airtime, laterals, and a surprise tunnel. The beginning of the ride features a "split lift" which carries the train halfway to the ride's full height, turns around, and travels the rest of the way up directly over the lower lift. This opening is unique and actually contributes to the fun.

3. TEXAS GIANT—Six Flags Over Texas, Arlington, Texas

The "masterpiece of mayhem" is one of the largest wooden roller coasters in the world. The large first drop leads to twisting, sharp dives in the first third, a double helix that wraps around and slices through the lift hill in the second third, and a finale of rabbit hops that winds around the entire main structure, taken at breathless speed. It features just about every good aspect ever designed into a wooden coaster.

4. ROAR—Six Flags Marine World, Vallejo, California

The design of this ride is a tribute to 1920s swirling masterpieces, with turns in each drop and drops in each turn. The passenger trains, replicas of the style vehicles used on those

1920s rides, really bring back a bygone era. Not only is this ride a trip down memory lane, but it's also an extreme thriller, with a track layout that criss-crosses itself eighteen times, and a relentless speed along a course that is so gnarled, the rider can't second guess it.

5. WILDCAT—Hersheypark, Hershey, Pennsylvania

This work of art was the first coaster designed by Great Coasters, International. It's a swirling, modern recreation of the great roller coaster thrills of the 1920s, featuring spiral drops, insane turns, relentless pacing—similar in style to our #4 choice, Roar, but in a totally unique layout that also pays homage to the way roller coasters used to be.

TOP FIVE STEEL COASTERS

1. SUPERMAN RIDE OF STEEL—Six Flags New England, Agawam, Massachusetts

Steel had always been the favored building material of looping roller coasters, but in 1989, it was discovered that steel was good for something else: the giant 200-foot-tall non-looping coaster, similar in design style to the beloved wooden coaster, but in a super-plus-size model. This is the ride that is the one to beat in the category of non-looping steel, as well as any other. The 221-foot-long drop at a 78-degree angle into an underground tunnel is only the beginning for this masterpiece. What follows are a series of large hills, an intense figure-eight, and a series of sharp rabbit hops for a finale. There isn't one moment on this ride that gives passengers a chance to catch their breath; it's *that* action-packed. The world's ultimate roller coaster, wood or steel.

2. MAGNUM XL-200—Cedar Point, Sandusky, Ohio

If Superman Ride of Steel is the pinnacle of giant steel roller coasters, this is the legend that started it all. The first full circuit coaster towering 200 feet, it remains one of the most thrilling on the planet, with deep drops at its start, a fascinating pretzel shaped turnaround, and a relentless series of rabbit hops that race to the finish line. Still produces one of the best adrenaline rushes of any coaster out there.

3. KUMBA—Busch Gardens Tampa Bay, Tampa, Florida

This giant looping coaster was built in 1992, and has a smoothness not seen before on this type of ride, along with new-fangled inversion elements also new to this type of attraction. The installation of Kumba included heavy landscaping, as well as the building up of the terrain below the track, making the ride appear to be sitting on a rolling hillside, when in fact it's on completely flat ground. The ride uses this new terrain elevation to feature several interesting moments, including a dive into an underground tunnel.

4. NITRO—Six Flags Great Adventure, Jackson, New Jersey

Not only is this ride the tallest roller coaster in the northeastern United States, but it's also the tallest and longest ride ever built at the park. You'll be amused by the height comparison signs on the way up the lift hill ("You have now reached the height of the Leaning Tower of Pisa"), and you'll be amazed by one of the best first drops in the business. A combination twister and out-and-back, the coaster combines all the best elements into one giant, thrilling package.

5. MILLENNIUM FORCE—Cedar Point, Sandusky, Ohio

The first park to build a full circuit coaster over 200 feet tall just *had* to build the first 300 footer, too, which they did in the year 2000. This sprawling monster features the world's best first drop, a full 300 feet at an 80-degree angle. The track following was designed more for speed than action, so it's a bit different in character from similar non-looping steel rides, but definitely contains a little of this here and a little of that there, and *a lot* of speed everywhere.

TOP FIVE RIDES

1. THE AMAZING ADVENTURES OF SPIDER-MAN—
Islands of Adventure, Orlando, Florida

   Amazing isn't even the word for this astonishing piece of entertainment. A 3-D virtual experience combined with vehicles actually moving along on a track puts you face to face with Spidey in ways you've never even dreamed of. This is actually more of a thrill ride than many roller coasters.

2. BACK TO THE FUTURE—Universal Studios Florida, Orlando, Florida

   Universal isn't kidding when they say "Ride The Movies". You're in your own DeLorean and you *will* feel as though you are rocketing through space and time. The action here is vigorous, making this one of the more action-packed rides in the world.

3. PERILOUS PLUNGE—Knott's Berry Farm, Buena Park, California

   You like roller coasters? You like water rides? Want to combine the two for a wet thrill? Then this is your ride. It's a giant sized version of the standard shoot-the-chute found at many theme parks, but it also features one heck of a steep drop to the pond below. In fact, the drop on this contraption is more frightening than *most* roller coasters.

4. WONDER WHEEL—Deno's Wonder Wheel Park, Brooklyn, New York

   Don't call this a ferris wheel. While it does feature cars that hang from the outer rim, just like any other ferris wheel, its meatier cars travel on a rail from the outer rim to the center of the wheel, swinging wildly, and making even experienced riders a bit nervous. A National Historic Landmark, and for good reason, in the heart of historic Coney Island.

5. HOUDINI'S GREAT ESCAPE—Six Flags Great Adventure, Jackson, New Jersey

An absolutely brilliant cheap thrill illusion ride experience. It features a pre-show explaining to guests how famed magician Harry Houdini intended to come back from the grave, and then places them in a room where Harry begins to wreak havoc. Are both the room and you really spinning upside down? Are those gravitational forces all faked? You decide. Seating here contains two long benches on either side, so you get to see the other half of riders freaking out, which is part of the overall experience.

TOP FIVE ATTRACTIONS

1. HAUNTED HOUSE—Knoebels Amusement Resort, Elysburg, Pennsylvania

The best classic dark ride in the United States. Built by the park staff, it contains many different rooms, and your little car will travel from living room, to attic, to basement, and even outside to the "graveyard". Scares galore, with something happening at every turn.

2. NOAH'S ARK—Kennywood, West Mifflin, Pennsylvania

Walk-through funhouses were once an amusement park staple. But since we live in a litigious society ("I tripped on my own shoelaces and it's *your fault*"), they've all but disappeared. Mercifully, instead of removing this classic, the park actually restored it and added to it, making it a long, elaborate masterpiece, filled with old-style walk-through stunts, plus some new ones that are quite wonderful. A *must* for anyone in the park, at least several times.

3. TERMINATOR 2 3-D—Universal Studios, Orlando, Florida

Visit Cyberdine, and become part of the terrifying plot of the Terminator movies in this attraction that combines a 3-D film, live action actors, and a few amazing 4-D surprises. A really stunning experience not to be missed.

4. MYSTERY LODGE—Knott's Berry Farm, Buena Park, California

    This is part live action show, part special effects extravaganza. Old Storyteller takes you on a journey deep into the heart of our Native American history that is fabulously entertaining, moving, and awe-inspiring. Simply beautiful in every way.

5. EIFFEL TOWER—Paramount's Kings Island, Cincinnati, Ohio; Paramount's Kings Dominion, Doswell, Virginia

    At 330 feet, this is a one-third scale replica of the real thing, and it is at the center of the park. It has two levels of observation decks, with one at 275 feet up, the more popular of the pair. The glass-sided elevators that take you to the top provide a nice view, and the well-trained attendant will give you the history of both the real Eiffel Tower and the replica. At the top, with the park spread out around you and the cool summer breezes blowing, you'll find yourself amazed that such peace and tranquility can be attained in the center of a giant theme park, even if you do hear the occasional screams from the thrill riders echoing through the air.

THE
PARK GUIDE

4

THE NORTHEAST

CONEY ISLAND
DORNEY PARK
HERSHEYPARK
KENNYWOOD
KNOEBELS AMUSEMENT RESORT
SIX FLAGS GREAT ADVENTURE
SIX FLAGS NEW ENGLAND

CONEY ISLAND

Surf Avenue to Boardwalk
Between West 8th Street and West 20th Street
Brooklyn, New York 11224
Admission: Varies; see particular attraction listings
Operating Schedule: Palm Sunday through October. Parks open at noon,
    other attractions vary.

Park History

Coney Island is the world-famous amusement area, the birthplace of
what we know today as the modern amusement park. The world's
first roller coaster was built here, as well as many other rides that

have morphed into today's modern screamers. And of course, America's favorite snack food, the good old hot dog, also originates from here. The first gated, pay-one-price park was built here, and the three main parks that lured people in for decades (Steeplechase, Luna, and Dreamland) certainly provided copycats like Walt Disney with the basis for his very own parks, which came much later. It is safe to say that the entire theme park industry was born right on this southern shore of Brooklyn.

Today's Coney Island is less of an amusement park and more of a neighborhood comprised of many separate entertainment venues; there are two amusement parks, rides that operate as stand-alone attractions on city street corners, an aquarium, a minor league baseball stadium, and, of course, the four mile Riegelman Boardwalk, one of the world's longest. The single most popular attraction at Coney Island is the legendary Cyclone, still considered one of the world's greatest wooden roller coasters after three-quarters of a century in existence.

Major Attractions

Cyclone—National Historic Landmark wooden roller coaster

Wonder Wheel—National Historic Landmark ferris wheel

Beach and Boardwalk—Four miles of beautiful beach, on one of the world's longest boardwalks

Getting There

By car: Take the Belt Parkway to exit 7S, and follow Ocean Parkway until it curves right and becomes Surf Avenue. The attractions will be on your left.

By public transportation: Several subway and bus lines reach the heart of Coney Island. At press time, the main subway station at Stillwell Avenue and Surf Avenue is being completely rebuilt, and train service is subject to heavy changes. Check with New York City's Metropolitan Transit Authority (MTA) to find out which lines are in operation at the time of your visit.

Planning to Go

Coney Island amusement parks offer free admission, but each ride is pay as you go, from $2 to $5, which can add up. Both main parks offer a pay-one-price or package deal during weekdays, but there are limits to the amounts of trips you can take on certain rides. One way to avoid this is to call Astroland, the main park you'll be visiting (718-265-2100), and book a group. The park offers any group of fifteen or more an unlimited wristband good for five hours during weekdays, or four on weekends, at an astonishingly low price of $8.99 per person. Lunch can be added for a few dollars more. And except for two or three other rides in the area, all the rides you'll want to go on are part of Astroland. Remember, you must have fifteen or more people to take advantage of this rate, so gather up friends, family, and neighbors, and get ready to roll.

Beginning the Day

If arriving by car, you have three parking options. One is to find metered parking on the street, which will be difficult if you arrive after 11 A.M. (the parks open at noon). The price for metered parking is 25 cents per half-hour, and the meters only fill to two hours, so if this is the course you choose, don't forget to keep going back to feed the meter (you'll get a pricey parking ticket if you don't). You can also park in the Keyspan Stadium parking lot, from $8 to $12, depending on the day and schedule of events throughout the island. Parking lot attendants will ask what you'll be doing that day—if you say you're attending a game or special event, they'll charge you a higher rate. *Always* tell them you're just going to the beach for the day. The third option is to park in the New York

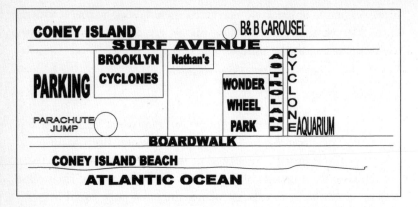

Aquarium lot. It's priced high at about $16, but includes one free adult admission to the Aquarium. If any members of your group are planning to visit the aquarium, this might be the way to go.

Attractions

The New York Aquarium

Boardwalk at West 8th Street
Brooklyn, New York 11224
718-265-FISH
Admission: $10 adult, $6 children

First opened in 1957, this is a full service aquarium, with exhibits, shows, and everything else an aquarium is known for. If you're planning to go to the aquarium, you'll want to arrive early; opening is at 9 or 10 A.M., depending on season. You'll have a few hours to see all that's offered, then head on over to the rides. It's a great, slow build up to what lies ahead.

Beach and Boardwalk

Brighton Beach to Seagate
Brooklyn, New York 11224
Admission: Free

The free beach and boardwalk has been entertaining people for almost two centuries. It's safe, relatively clean for a public beach located in a major city, and can actually be quite a peaceful experience. Swimming is permitted in areas where lifeguards are on duty. The area east of the amusement parks is where more local residents will be on the beach, so try heading there, as it will be far less crowded.

Astroland

1000 Surf Avenue
Brooklyn, New York 11224
718-265-2100
Admission: Pay-one-price $14.99 (weekdays only)

This is the main amusement park on Coney Island, and is home to the National Historic Landmark Cyclone. As mentioned above, a group of fifteen or more can book a special rate of $8.99 per person, which offers unlimited rides on most everything in the park for a five hour period.

If you don't have enough people to take advantage of the group rate, normal pricing is as follows: Pay-one-price wristbands are available in two different sessions (noon to 6 P.M. and 5 P.M. to 10 P.M.) on non-holiday weekdays only for $14.99 (there are several ride limit restrictions with this purchase). Other times, rides are priced pay-as-you-go, and cost from $2 to $5. You'll be buying tickets at each ride (ticket booths are located at the entrances to individual rides), but *take care* with your cash and count your change! These ticket sellers have been known to short-change customers or take advantage of the fact that most are in an excited rush and leave their change behind.

Time constraints can cut down on the value a park goer receives for his money (waiting in lines are the main villain responsible for this). Astroland guests need not worry—the park was named by the *Wall Street Journal* as the place to go for less wait-in-line time and more ride time, beating out every other park in the United States. Therefore, your time spent at Astroland will be filled with hoots and hollers, not with bored-to-tears downtime.

You owe it to yourself to start your day at Astroland with a ride on the Cyclone. This magnificent creation, opened in 1927, gives the term "rough and tumble" an entirely new meaning. The Cyclone has its shortest lines when it first opens for the day, so that's a good time to check out this legend, but be warned: it always runs slower than usual when it first starts rolling for the day. You'll need to revisit it again later on to get more of its full fury.

Crossing the street to the main area of Astroland, you'll notice three adult rides right in the front of the park. All three operate in full Coney Island fashion, which means if a ride has a full speed ahead switch, it's used. While theme parks tend to tone down the speed or action of a ride, Coney likes to rev it up as much as it can. Therefore, the innocent looking rocking pirate ship at the very front of Astroland, which you've seen in dozens of amusement parks, suddenly becomes a high-octane thrill ride, swinging so high as to be almost perpendicular to the ground. Don't miss this ride. (A note on all of Astroland's spinning rides: A theme park will usually give a one or two minute ride on them—here, you'll get to ride for as long as the operator feels like keeping you on it, sometimes five minutes or more, and you may find yourself cringing in your seat wishing for the motion to stop. You've been warned!)

Next to the pirate ship is another familiar amusement park staple, the Enterprise. This swinging car, upside-down device can be a boring experience at most parks, but at Astroland, it is operated in a way that makes the cars rock while they are soaring into the sky, producing a very welcome additional thrill.

The third ride in the front of the park is the Power Surge, which offers guests an experience that is somewhat akin to riding a ferris wheel during a hurricane. It is a flashy, high-tech gadget, and its cars spin in five different directions at one time, as passengers' feet dangle from the ski-lift style seats. Don't miss it.

Next up is Dante's Inferno, a classic, old-fashioned ride-through dark ride. It's mostly a trip through the dark with a few hilariously bad moving figures and cheesy stunts. It is very popular, however, and always has one of the longest lines in the park. Only do it if the line is short, and keep in mind that in its present state, it's not scary—it's hokey, and therefore very suitable for every member of the family.

You'll next encounter Break Dance. If you like spinning rides, this one is a must. It's been given awards as one of the world's best "spin and pukes." This evil machine consists of spinning cars on arms that also spin, all mounted on a huge sloping disk, which *also* spins, and is manually operated by very knowledgeable park employees to maximize its potential. *Everyone* staggers away from it at ride's end. You'll get a test spin before the actual full motion of the ride begins, and don't be embarrassed to raise your hand so they'll stop the ride and let you off—you won't be the first, and you certainly won't be the last.

Right next to this most insane park attraction is perhaps the most sedate. The Astrotower is a rotating observation deck which rises to a height of 253 feet, the second tallest ride at Coney Island. It can be intimidating to some because of its precarious height and the clear plexiglass windows that separate you from the ground far, far below, but the view is amazing, and it's a great place to just sit for a spell and see all of New York City and its magnificent harbor.

Now it's time to cool off. The park's historic water flume was only the third such attraction ever built in the world. This water coaster has a few hills, a splashy finale, and is the most popular ride in the park. It's very suitable for all members of the family.

If you like bumper cars, Astroland's are among the best. They are fast, without any sort of center guide, and they can get totally out of control. You'll know you've ridden a bumper car ride when you're through. The line can be long for this ride, though, and the slow loading and dispatch intervals can drive a person crazy. It's very possibly part of the plan, so that you build up some aggression and let it loose when the cars start to rampage around the course.

Astroland's kiddie park contains several adult rides: Scrambler, Tilt-a-Whirl, and Carousel. They are perfect for adults who want to ride with their children. The selection of kiddie rides offers various forms of thrills, and there's even a kiddie coaster. The fire engine ride in the park is a classic original manufactured by the Mangels company, formerly located right around the corner from the Cyclone. They were one of the world's long-standing ride manufacturers and were located in Coney Island. Their old factory is now home to the Department of Motor Vehicles.

The park offers food at two separate locations, one on the boardwalk, and one on the corner of West 10th Street and Surf Avenue. Although not the same building, this Surf Avenue location is where Feltman's Restaurant once stood. Owner Charles Feltman invented the hot dog (Nathan ripped him off), and the hot dogs sold from this Astroland site are considered by many to be the best hot dog offered anywhere on Coney Island. Don't miss them (and don't forget to sample the fresh cut french fries while you're at it).

Deno's Wonder Wheel Park

Boardwalk and West 12th Street
Brooklyn, New York 11224
718-372-2592
Admission: Pay-as-you-go

The main claim to fame for this park is the one and only Wonder Wheel. At 150 feet tall, it's not only one of the largest ferris wheels in the world; it is also the most distinctive, because of its swinging cars. Look closely at this awesome structure, and you'll notice that each red and blue car is on an oval-shaped track. As the wheel raises your car higher off the ground, you find yourself suddenly riding a roller coaster as the car, mounted on wheels, begins to roll along the track towards the inside of the wheel. While you're at your highest point, you ride as if on a regular ferris wheel again, but coming back down, you roll along the track again, and this time, it's even more precarious, since your car is now swinging towards the outside of the wheel. It can be a breathtaking experience, and although you'll only get two revolutions, it's well worth the $4. You can select a traditional ferris wheel experience by choosing a white car; they are fixed to the perimeter of the wheel and don't swing.

Coney Island's magnificent Wonder Wheel. (*Credit: courtesy of Deno's Wonder Wheel Park*)

Next door to Wonder Wheel is another Coney Island classic dark ride, known as Spook-a-rama. This is yet one more great example of cheap, cheesy, but hilarious old-fashioned dark ride-through. You'll never be scared, but you'll get a good laugh.

The park offers a package deal good for all five adult rides at a price of $14.99, but you won't need to purchase that, since the previously mentioned rides are the only ones worth checking out.

Deno's has a boardwalk-level kiddie land, which is a bit nicer than Astroland's since it's right up on the boardwalk (Astroland's is at street level). The rides are about the same at each, but the location is far more charming. Deno's Wonder Wheel Park also offers a well-trained staff of young adults, who tend to be more family-friendly than the flotsam and jetsam who work next door.

B and B Carousel
Surf Avenue and West 12th Street
Brooklyn, New York 11224
Admission: $3

At this location since 1939—but originally constructed in 1912—
the actual carousel is the oldest operating ride in all of Coney
Island. It is also one of only three carousels in the world where you
can still "catch the brass ring." This is the last remaining attraction
on the north side of Surf Avenue, and it sits on a site that was once
the home of the Elephant Hotel (a huge structure built in the shape
of an elephant). Later, it was home to both Sea Lion Park (the
world's first enclosed, pay-one-price amusement park) and Luna
Park, a grand affair that was the basis for Disneyland.

Coney Island Museum and Sideshow
Surf Avenue and West 12th Street
Brooklyn, New York 11224
718-372-5159
Admission: Museum, $1, Sideshow, $5

The museum, which has its entrance on Surf Avenue, contains
many rare artifacts from old Coney Island, and is definitely worth a
stop. For the meager sum of 99 cents, you can browse the collection
of rare photos, postcards, and trinkets on display. The prize exhibit
at the museum is a horse from the famed Steeplechase ride, and
you'll enjoy viewing yourself in the funhouse distortion mirrors.
The museum is still being constructed, so it will look a bit disor-
ganized, but that's why the price is so cheap.

The Sideshow, in the same building as the museum and with an
entrance on West 12th Street, is a continuously running half-hour
show with mixed degrees of entertainment value. It can be fun to
watch, but also a tad on the amateurish side at times. If you actually
pay the full price of $5 to see it, you may not exactly be thrilled
with yourself. Therefore, don't just wander in and buy a ticket.
What they don't want you to know is that about every 15–20 minutes, the management does a little preview of the sideshow on a
stage set up in the street out front. They then announce that if you

buy your ticket right then and there, you'll be given a "one time only" special rate of $3, and that this special price will expire within five minutes. This is commonly called ballyhoo, and is one of the most tried and true Coney Island tricks on record. Therefore, if for some reason you can't go see the sideshow at that very moment for the discount price, not to worry. It will be offered again in a few minutes, and again, and again. Just wait for the preview to begin and the announcement to be made.

Both the museum and sideshow have gift shops. Unless you absolutely must have an item that is sold at either one, avoid both, as all items sold in them are marked up ridiculously. And while the t-shirts are exclusive designs, most of the other items aren't, and can be found throughout Coney Island, sometimes for about half the price.

El Dorado Bumper Cars

Surf Avenue
Brooklyn, New York 11224
Admission: $3.50

A classic bumper car ride, but with a twist. The attraction is located inside an arcade, and is fully indoors. Fantastic lights and a booming sound system are utilized in conjunction with today's pop music to create a bumping discotheque where the cars pulsate along the floor to the beat of the music.

Coney Island Batting Range and Go Kart City

Stillwell Avenue and The Bowery
Brooklyn, New York 11224
718-449-1200
Admission: Pay-as-you-go

A collection of go-karts, batting ranges, and bumper boats all designed to encourage active participation in the fun. Adjacent to the complex is a more passive entertainment—a thrill ride known as Top Spin, a flipping, inverting ride that is operated in "insane" mode.

Brooklyn Cyclones Baseball

1904 Surf Avenue
Brooklyn, New York 11224
718-449-8497
Admission: Tickets are priced from $6 to $12

Keyspan Park, a beautiful new ballfield, was built in 2001, and is home to the Brooklyn Cyclones—named for the world-famous roller coaster just a few blocks to the east. The Brooklyn Cyclones is a minor league team that serves as a farm team to the New York Mets, and the games themselves are as exciting as any minor league baseball game can be. The location—right on the boardwalk, with the sea breezes blowing in the fans' faces and the sights and sounds of the rides and attractions just beyond the outfield wall—definitely adds to the ambience in a way that no other ball park can claim.

A word of advice if you're planning to attend a game: The Brooklyn Cyclones heralded the return of baseball to Brooklyn after an absence of over forty years following the Dodgers' move to Los Angeles. Tickets sell out regularly, so advance purchases are advised. You may luck out and be able to buy tickets the day of the game, but only plan on doing that if you don't particularly care if you see a game the day of your visit or not.

Another word: The Brooklyn Cyclones know they're a big deal. Pricing at the stadium for souvenirs, food, etc. is *extreme*, about level with what you'd pay at any major league sports venue. Be prepared. Grab something to eat before the game, as the $4.50 hot dog is only $2 a block away. Only buy souvenirs if you must have them (resisting a purchase will be difficult, though, they have extremely nice stuff for sale!).

Parachute Jump

Boardwalk at Keyspan Park
Brooklyn, New York 11224

The world famous "Eiffel Tower of Brooklyn" is currently undergoing a restoration process. At press time, it's completely deconstructed, having rust removed from its steel girders and new rivets and bolts placed. There's a plan for it to be fully operational again (the first time since 1964), with a grand re-opening in 2004.

Nathan's Famous

Stillwell And Surf Avenues
Brooklyn, New York 11224
Admission: Hot dogs are priced at $2

This is the original Nathan's, in the original location. Nathan Handwerker was employed by Charles Feltman, the true inventor of the hot dog. After he had saved enough money, Handwerker branched off and opened his own hot dog stand. He charged five cents per dog, which cut in half the price that Feltman was charging just a few blocks away. Nathan assumed that his lower prices—along with his location almost directly across the street from the Stillwell Avenue subway station—would be a no-brainer for his success. But people stayed away, assuming that his lower prices meant inferior quality, so he was not an immediate success. One day, he assembled a group of local street bums, dressed them in surgical whites and lab coats, and had them fill up the counter of his establishment, under a sign that said "If doctors eat here, it must be good". The crowds fell for the scam, and Nathan's has been a Coney Island institution ever since.

These days, Nathan's is a major chain, and this location unfortunately does not live up to its reputation. If you must have a hot dog here, feel free to do so, just so you can tell everyone back home you've eaten at the original Coney Island Nathan's—but honestly, a Nathan's in any shopping mall is a better bet. And be aware, they do not have any type of combo meals here, and rarely do they accept coupons that are good at other Nathan's locations.

You should plan on ending the day at Coney Island with a spin on the Astrotower or Wonder Wheel, for the spectacular night time views, and then the Cyclone, to see just how rambunctious this creature is in the evening. One night-time attraction that shouldn't be missed is the free weekly fireworks display, offered every Friday throughout the summer, and perhaps the closest you'll ever get to *touching* fireworks. They are truly spectacular, and a perfect way to end a summer evening at this wonderful, magical place.

DORNEY PARK AND WILDWATER KINGDOM

3830 Dorney Park Road
Allentown, Pennsylvania
610-395-3724
www.dorneypark.com
Admission: $35 (regular season, less in spring and fall)
Operating Schedule: May through October. Park opens at 10 A.M.,
  with closing times varying throughout the season.

Park History

Dorney Park is one of the oldest continuously operated amusement parks in the country. It began life as a fishing weir back in the mid-nineteenth century, eventually adding rides, games and pavilions.

The park was privately owned and quite successful until 1995, when it was purchased by Cedar Fair, LP, a large corporate chain of theme and amusement parks. Subsequent upgrades and expansion have eliminated much of the old Dorney Park (and its old-fashioned charm), but the expansions added spectacular rides and upgraded facilities that turned the charming little local park into a major destination.

The park today is one of the better large park values, and it features a wooden coaster and a steel one that are both among the tallest in the world in their categories.

Major Attractions

Steel Force—200-foot-tall, non-looping steel roller coaster
Talon—Largest inverted roller coaster on the East Coast
Thunder Hawk—Classic wooden roller coaster
Thunder Canyon—Amazingly wet and wild river rapids ride

Getting There

By car: Take I-78 East to exit 54 or I-78 West to 54B. You can see the park from the highway. Follow the signs to the parking lot entrance. If you purchase a season pass to the park, you can use the separate entrance and special, preferred parking lot exclusively for season pass holders.

Planning to Go

This is one park that will not run the big roller coasters in heavy rain. Don't expect to apply the "rain rule" at this park, because you probably won't get a chance to ride anything you really want to. A very light rain will not shut rides down, so if that's what the forecast calls for, feel free to go.

Be sure to call the park and ask about discounts offered through local vendors. Fast food chains frequently offer coupons. There's also an after 4 P.M. discount on the price of admission, but more on that later. Early and late in the season, when the water park section of Dorney Park and Wildwater Kingdom is not open, the general admission is also heavily discounted, so you might want to plan to go during those times.

Beginning Your Day

The park opens at 10 A.M. Plan to arrive earlier than that, simply because the awkward, sloped parking lot begins filling up and eventually, cars that arrive late are put into the overflow lot, which is across a service road and is a *long* walk from the main entrance to the park. You don't want to park there, under any circumstances.

If you've decided to bring a picnic lunch, Dorney provides a free picnic pavilion just outside the main entrance, but space is first come, first served. You can actually put your belongings inside and save your space, or wait 'til lunchtime and take your chances. It might be a better idea to just plan to have a tailgate party at your car. The pavilion fills up quickly, and is not big enough to make it comfortable (it's free, after all).

As mentioned above, Dorney Park and Wildwater Kingdom is a member of the Cedar Fair, LP family of parks. A season pass purchased at one is good for admission to all parks within the chain (currently Cedar Point, Sandusky, Ohio; ValleyFair, Shakopee, Minnesota; Dorney Park and Wildwater Kingdom, Allentown, Pennsylvania; Worlds of Fun, Kansas City, Missouri; Knott's Berry Farm, Buena Park, California; and Michigan's Adventure, Muskegon, Michigan). If you plan to visit any of these parks in the same season, buy a season pass to the first one you plan to visit. (You must process the pass at the park for which you buy it, so buying it online from the park that sells it the cheapest won't help you unless you are planning to visit that same park before any others in the chain. You must have a processed pass to gain admittance to the other parks.) Dorney's season pass office is located in the main entrance plaza area, to the right of the admittance gate. Their pass price is about $80 and is neither the highest nor lowest price within the Cedar Fair chain.

Dorney Park and Wildwater Kingdom is a combination amusement park/water park. Both are included in the admission. The water park has an interesting effect on the amusement park—it

STEEL FORCE
THUNDERHAWK
LASER DOMINATOR HERCULES
WHITE WATER LANDING
MAIN ENTRANCE CAROUSEL CAMP SNOOPY
THUNDER CANYON
DORNEY PARK TO WILDWATER KINGDOM TALON

keeps the rides relatively line-free until late in the day on the sunniest days. While the water park offers some spectacular devices, if you really want to experience the amusement park, skip the water park. At Dorney, the usual rule of a park emptying out in the evening hours doesn't necessarily apply. As the water park closes, the guests who've spent the day there will come into the amusement park, and the lines will begin to build up to horrendous proportions as night falls. You can splash in the bathtub when you get home if you really want to get wet.

In the Park

Once inside the main gate, you'll face Dorney's classic carousel. Feel free to hop on board, as this is a fine beginning to the day, and the ride rarely has a considerable line.

Almost right over the carousel, screams from riders on the Talon inverted roller coaster shatter the peace and quiet of the more laid-back horses. If you've arrived in the park right at opening time, head from the carousel right down the main midway, turn right, and go directly for this orange and yellow monster, the largest inverted roller coaster on the East Coast. Since it's the first thing people see as they enter the park, it draws them all day like a magnet. You'll want to get on it as quickly as possible, so do it first thing. Talon seats riders in groups of four, with legs and feet dangling. Make sure your shoes are tied tightly before you board, and loose objects are not permitted. The view from the front row on any inverted coaster is always spectacular, as you're literally flying through the air with the ground rushing to meet you.

After being in the clutches of Talon, you need to head right back down the midway toward the carousel again. At the carousel, turn right and head on down the hill to the lower section of the park. You're heading for Steel Force, one of the world's tallest steel roller coasters, and one of the best. It's literally all the way in the back of the park, and while most guests trickle onto rides as they stumble across them, you're on a mission.

Riding the rails of Steel Force with the tranquil Swan Boats on the left. (*Credit: Paul De Santis*)

Steel Force is 200 feet of pure power, a mile-long course that spreads from one end of the park to the other. Along the course, riders encounter a 205-foot drop into an underground tunnel, a second drop of 161 feet, a mind-numbing helix, and a series of air-time-producing rabbit hops that make the ending of the ride as good as the beginning. It's equally as good in the front of the train as it is in the back, and you'll want to ride it multiple times. Feel free to ride this sensational giant for as long as the line stays down.

After you've had your fill of Steel Force, it would be a good idea to check out the line on Laser, the park's sit down looper. Frequently, only one train is operational, and the lines can be very long. In theory, you've beaten the crowds to this section of the park, so Laser shouldn't be too crowded. It's a short ride, and while it's very good, you probably won't feel compelled to set any marathon records on it. Now it's time to head to a classic wooden roller coaster experience.

Thunder Hawk, the park's smaller wooden roller coaster, runs along the lower section of the park near Steel Force. It appears to be a real pussycat. It isn't. This rambunctious machine has out-of-seat-popping airtime and side-to-side laterals galore, as most wooden coasters from the 1920s do. It rarely builds up a line during the daytime hours. However, one bad by-product of this short line is that when there are few riders, the operators block off the rear of the train, forcing everyone to sit in the front. This is usually fine, as Thunder Hawk delivers the goods a bit better in the front. However, you might want to also experience the back. If so, you'll have to check back at a point when the queue is a little fuller, and therefore warranting a full train's worth of riders.

Next, check out Dominator. This launching tower ride offers two different experiences. On one tower, you're thrust from the ground to a height of 165 feet, and then thrust down in one fell swoop. Your vehicle then bounces a few times before it settles to the ground. It's a pure adrenaline rush. The second tower climbs slowly to the top, hangs there at a height of 175 feet for a few minutes, and then is thrust down, after which it attains the same bouncing finale as the first tower. Dominator is completely operated by air pressure, and is smooth beyond compare. The queue line is split into two sections, one for the launch-up tower and one for the launch-down tower. Arrows (one up and one down) point the way to each line, so make sure you choose the one you want. You won't be able to switch later on.

Having done five of the park's major rides now, you can start to slow down. Or, you can choose to get wet. The park offers two water rides that are actually worth waiting for. They are both located in the amusement park, near the entrance path to the water park in the upper section/entrance area. Thunder Canyon is one of the best river rapids rides in existence, and is a thoroughly soaking experience. With rapids rides, you usually either get spinning rapids that splash over the side of the boat, or waterfalls that pour over your head into the boat. Thunder Canyon offers both, and nothing you wear on the ride will remain dry. White Water Landing is a shoot-the-chutes ride, but very tall and with a hill that is as steep as any roller coaster. The splash at the bottom is huge, and it soaks riders and spectators, as well.

It's still early, and if Hercules—the huge wooden coaster behind White Water Landing—hasn't built up a line, hop on board. This ride offers a mixed bag of thrills. While it begins with a fifty-five-foot triple twisting drop out of the station, and is followed by a 150-foot plunge down the natural hillside the park resides on, Hercules quickly turns into a slow, meandering junior coaster. Ironically, the very hillside that allows Hercules to have such good moments at the beginning also prevents it from having anything too fantastic at the end. Following the huge drop, the coaster must make it all the way back up the hill, and unfortunately, the design has it remaining up there, never returning to the valley which is the location for the most furious part of the ride. Most of the remaining hills on the ride are not more than twenty feet high, and the coaster train has used up so much energy to return to the top of the hillside that it barely has enough speed to make it through the rest of the course. It's just not a world-class coaster experience, so only ride it if it has no line.

You've just taken a whirlwind tour of the park's major rides. Everything else in the park is standard fare, available in most parks, and unless you feel the need to jump aboard one of these common spinning contraptions, only do so if there is no line. There are, however, a few rides and attractions you shouldn't miss.

The smallish Giant Gondola Wheel near the main entrance to the park is not exceptionally tall, but its location on the very top of the park's hillside offers a tremendous view of the entire park. It's a pleasant, relaxing few minutes, suitable for the entire family.

The Zephyr train, located in the lower section of the park, is also one of the parks remaining classic rides, dating back to the Great Depression, and a solid example of old-time amusement devices. The miniature cabins on the train do indeed allow adults to ride. It's a far better train experience than the Cedar Creek Cannonball, which is located near the main entrance and was shortened so much by the installation of Talon that riding is now pointless.

The Monster, a spinning, up-and-down octopus-style ride located near the Zephyr train, is another old-fashioned ride experience, dating from the 1960s. This one is operated in a way that avoids any severe spinning, so feel free to take all members of the family on board.

Thunder Creek Mountain is a water flume ride, its course carved into the same hillside that Hercules occupies. It's got a few rare moments for a flume, including rapids, water curtains, a few water tricks, and a great drop down the hillside. It almost always has a line, however, so you might want to check back periodically to make sure you're not spending an hour waiting for it.

For kids, Dorney Park offers Camp Snoopy, a full-fledged kiddie land that that has a Peanuts character theme. It's a large area near the main entrance, and it offers plenty of shade and lots of rides for the little ones. Adjacent to it is a Wild Mouse, the zig-zagging style coaster that was popular in the 1950s and has recently been staging a comeback. This Wild Mouse is not one of the best of the new models, however, so only ride it if the line is short.

Food is the usual park fare. If you decide against bringing a picnic lunch of your own, select the Red Garter Saloon. This is Dorney Park's full service restaurant, and it has a decent selection of food at prices that won't exactly break the bank. What makes eating here even more attractive is that there is a stage show, usually featuring a musical review, and some of the talent that has appeared on Dorney Park stages has been nothing less than spectacular.

Speaking of shows, the Main Stage in the park, located near Dominator, usually has two different musical reviews, and again, while there might be an off note or two from a singer here or there, you just may be blown away by the performers you'll see on the stage. Cedar Fair holds national auditions for their in-park shows, and very talented performers have been known to appear.

If you're in the park all day, you'll notice the crowds growing around dinner time. The park offers an after-4 P.M. discount admission, and the water park empties out at around this time. The trend for this new influx of park guests is to head to the major rides, which you've already conquered during the day. The evening hours might be the best time to hit some of the more common rides in the park (no one runs out of the water park when it closes and heads directly for the tilt-a-whirl). Evening is also the best time to be in a park, as the temperature cools down, the lights heat up, and the true magic that is an amusement park goes full-throttle. Dorney Park is no exception. The park is beautiful at night, and it can be very calming.

Your day at Dorney Park is just about over. The traffic jam getting out of the park has already begun, and it will be that way for quite a while. (There are only two ways out of the parking lot, and one of them is used only by season pass holders. Both exits lead directly to the main road outside the park, hence the traffic build up.) Fortunately, Dorney Park allows guests to get in line right up 'til the posted closing time of the park. Now you may be thinking, "I have avoided lines all day, why do I want to get on one now?", but the logic here is that you'll wait on line and have a thrilling experience, instead of being in a car "waiting on line," only for it to lead to the long ride home. That's really no choice, is it?

HERSHEYPARK

100 West Hersheypark Drive
Hershey, Pennsylvania 17033
1-800-HERSHEY
www.hersheypark.com
Admission: $35
Operating Schedule: May through September, opens 10 A.M., with varying
    closing times.

Park History

Milton Hershey, founder of Hershey Chocolates, built this classic amusement park as part of the resort town that also bears his name. During the mid-1970s, the park was transformed into a major theme park, with certain areas retaining a classic, traditional park atmosphere. Today, it is world-renowned as one of the most family-oriented theme parks in America, and one of the favorites. Recent park expansion has added an entirely new themed area to the park, patterned after the kind of classic American midway from which the park originated.

Major Attractions

Lightning Racer—Dual-track, dueling wooden roller coaster
Wildcat—Severely twisted wooden roller coaster
Great Bear—Steel inverted coaster
Tidal Force—Giant version of shoot-the-chutes water ride

Getting There

In central Pennsylvania, follow interstate 81 to exit 28 (if traveling west) or exit 26 (if traveling east). Follow the signs to Hersheypark Drive, which is about ten minutes south of the exits.

Planning to Go

All park literature states that the hours of operation may be affected by weather. This policy will only apply to severe weather, so if it's just cloudy with a chance of light rain, the park will be open, and most likely for the hours posted for that particular day. Some rides may be affected by weather, but most likely they will be open periodically, at the very least.

The pay-one-price admission to the park is actually moderate, compared to others. There are plenty of coupons available at fast food restaurants for discounts, so be sure to call the park to ask which ones you can pick up on your way there. Burger King frequently offers deals, so that's a good one to try.

One very attractive admission policy at Hersheypark is the "preview" policy. Arrive at the park three hours before it closes, purchase your full-price next day ticket, and you'll be permitted to enter the park for the rest of the evening. The reason this is a beneficial way to get acquainted with the park is that, since it is the epitome of the regional family theme park, the evening hours here are not nearly as crowded as the daytime hours. You'll be amazed at how much you can do in those short hours before closing time.

Another attractive way to visit the park is to purchase a late admission ticket. For just a little more than half price, you can enter the park later in the day (the time depends on what time the park closes that evening) and enjoy all the attractions. Again, the park empties out quite considerably in the evening hours, and you'll be able to accomplish quite a bit. If you only have limited time to spend in the park, save it for later in the day when you can take advantage of this policy.

This is a resort town, and Hershey owns and operates many of its own hotels adjacent to the park. The evening hours in the park will be quite a bit more crowded on Fridays and Saturdays because of this, but Sunday evenings—as weekenders are heading home—will be most pleasurable.

Speaking of hotels, all the Hershey hotels offer discount packages that include theme park tickets, but you can also get discounts on tickets from various other hotels near the Hershey Resort. Call the park for details.

Beginning Your Day

Hersheypark has a large parking lot, and you just might find yourself parked miles from the main entrance. The park offers tram service to and from the front gate, but if you'd like to return to your car, this can be time consuming. When entering the parking lot, stay to the left, and try to park in the lot nearest to the Hershey Arena. This will put you as close to the main entrance as possible.

If you arrive in the morning, close to park opening time, forego Hershey's Chocolate World, which is just outside the main entrance. You can actually leave the park (don't forget to get your hand stamped) and do it mid-day. This history of chocolate making and, in particular, Hershey's chocolate, is fascinating, and you won't want to miss it.

However, the best bang for the buck, the aforementioned "preview" ticket, will give you a full day and a half to enjoy the park. Simply arrive just after noon, and hit Chocolate World first. This is a dark ride, and you may want to enjoy it a few times. You'll even get a chocolate sample upon exiting the ride. Best of all, the admission to this attraction is free! Chocolate World also contains various other attractions, shops, and restaurants that could all easily occupy an afternoon—and the chocolate available, Hershey products all, is about the freshest, most delicious chocolate you'll ever taste (the standard Hershey Bar, purchased here, will have your mouth watering). If you pace yourself properly and enjoy Chocolate World and Tudor Square (the shopping village surrounding the main entrance), you'll be ready to head into the theme park just about the time when the preview tickets go on sale for that day. You'll then be able to enjoy rides in the evening, with still another full day to go.

In the Park

Once inside the main gate, you'll be in Rhineland, a shopping village containing park souvenirs as well as beautiful gift items. The best time to shop is midday, so bypass all the shops and head straight through to Carousel Circle (not a typo, the park really does spell "carrousel" this way). Once past the gorgeous antique horses that reside on this well-crafted machine, head to the left, right through Music Box Way and Pioneer Village, until you find yourself in Midway America.

Midway America is the newest themed area within Hersheypark, and it also contains two of the park's major attractions, Wildcat and Lightning Racer. Head directly down the midway to the end, until you are greeted by the imposing structure of the Racer's Loading Station. Patterned after classic midway structures, this building houses the boarding point of the park's newest hit—Lightning Racer, a dual-tracked, dueling wooden roller coaster. If you get here

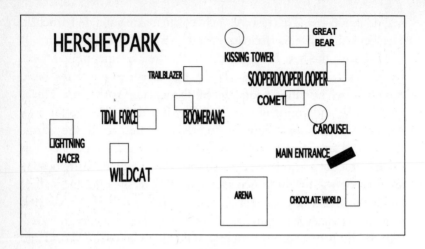

early in the morning, you'll arrive before most of the crowds, so feel free to hop onboard both sides of this masterpiece and take a few spins. It's family-friendly (meaning not only for the strong of heart), but is also very thrilling. The two tracks race side-by-side at times, but also separate and pass each other in near-head-on-collisions. This is a very creative ride, and the vehicles in use on it are designed to resemble those that were in operation during the Roaring Twenties—the decade often referred to as the "golden age" of roller coasters.

After you've ridden Lightning Racer a few times, feel free to try out some of the other pleasures that Midway America has to offer. There's a giant gondola ferris wheel, a few spinning rides, and a modern Wild Mouse—a throwback to the 1950s style, seat-of-your-pants roller coasters that, while small in size, pack a big wallop. The section also offers a modern version of a classic Whip—the rolling, snapping oval-shaped device that has been around for decades. If you're a fan of classic rides, though, don't even think this one will be bringing back any memories. It looks like a Whip, rides like a Whip, smells like a Whip, and tastes like a Whip, but it just *isn't* a Whip, and it may just leave a bad taste in your mouth.

The twisted track of Wildcat. (*Credit: Hersheypark*)

The next stop on your agenda has to be the awesome Wildcat—
another classic-style, wooden roller coaster. Like the slightly newer
Lightning Racer, it is designed to resemble the swirling giants of
the 1920s. This ride is sometimes ferocious, and is a bit more rambunctious than the Racer at the other end of the midway. It's perhaps a bit more hardcore thrill ride than anything else.

If you're ready to get a bit wet, Midway America has a ride you
won't want to miss. Roller Soaker is a suspended roller coaster water
ride, featuring four passenger cars that hang below the track, all
affixed with water guns allowing passengers to soak passersby on
the ground and in the queue-line. Be warned, though, that on the
ground, your human targets can strike back with their own water

blasters, so it's a 100% chance that *everyone* will get saturated. It's a fun ride, designed to be interactive.

If you're still raring to get wet, the neighboring Pioneer Village area contains Canyon River Rapids, a standard raging rapids ride, and the towering Tidal Force, one of the tallest shoot-the-chutes rides in the world. The tidal wave created when the boat splashes down the huge hill will amaze you. The area also contains a standard selection of spinning rides. *Only* ride them if they have a minimal line. They are not unique to this park, and you don't want to waste any time and perhaps miss the good stuff. Another ride you shouldn't spend too much time waiting for is the all-too-prolific boomerang shuttle coaster, here known as Sidewinder. While this model runs smoother than others, it's just about everywhere, and if you've ridden one, you've ridden them all.

Work your way down the hilly path next to Sidewinder and, with kids in tow, head for Trailblazer. It's one of those family "runaway mine train" coasters—short and not very thrilling, but perfect for the entire family to ride and enjoy together. If you're not travelling with kids and have a high thrill quotient, you won't be missing a thing if you skip it.

Next up at the top of a hillside, is Mine Town. You'll be sure to find it by searching out the tall observation tower known as the "Kissing Tower"—it's located at the highest point of the park. Located here is Great Bear, a steel inverted outside-looping coaster, which may look daunting to a few, but is in fact, very family-oriented and gentle (a trait that many of the rides at Hersheypark share). You'll sit in ski-lift-style seats that hang below the track, which will spin you through four inversions. The best part of the ride is when it flies over spectators in other sections of the park. (A little piece of info about the queue line: when it gets to the bridge that enters the station, the line is designed to split in two—the left is for the front seat, and the right is for all other seats. Don't get caught on an extra long line because people aren't paying attention to this—make them move!) Also located here is the Coal Cracker water flume. It's not by any means a major ride, and contains only one hill, which you will *not* get tremendously soaked on—meaning it's good for a splash, and for families who want to get wet but not soaked.

Move on down the hill past Great Bear and Coal Cracker, and walk right under your next objective—the sooperdooperLooper, a small, single looping traditional-riding roller coaster. This one is fun, and again, not aggressive enough to terrorize even the meekest family member. Unless the park is packed, it rarely has a significant line, and you might just find yourself riding over and over just because it's so *cute*.

You've now made your way completely around the park and have found yourself in Comet Hollow, home to the park's 1946 classic wooden roller coaster, Comet. This ride has an out and back design, featuring over a dozen consecutive hills known as "rabbit hops." It is a very clever design, which reaches a height of seventy-eight feet but features a first drop of ninety-six (the drop dips down into a small valley containing a creek). Nothing to worry about, however; Comet is merely fast and relentless, and it doesn't have anything nerve-shattering. When you've exited Comet, you'll find yourself face to face with the Carousel again, which means you've now been on just about every major ride in the park. It's time to slow down, and check out what you've missed.

One of the nicest things about Hersheypark is that each section contains both kiddie rides and adult rides. Familes don't have to drag the children around with nothing for them to experience if the older members of your group want to go on the thrillers. Kiddie rides are found in Carousel Circle, Midway America, Pioneer Village, Mine Town, and most abundantly in Music Box Way, right beside their larger versions. It's a total pleasure to be able to go from ride to ride and have something for everyone.

There are many places to eat within the park. The food has typical theme park prices, and is actually not bad. Several of the seasonal shows are also entertaining, and a few of them are presented within eating establishments, so try to match your dining time with show time and you'll get the best of both worlds.

Another great feature of the park is that, as night falls, the crowds thin out considerably (remember, this is a family park, and the families with younger kids will be leaving before park closing to put the little ones to bed). Ride lines, especially in Midway America, will be quite short in the last operating hour of the park, and rides such as Wildcat and Lightning Racer will be yours.

The shops in Rhineland remain open past park closing, as exiting guests complete their shopping for the day. Don't forget to get some unique Hersheypark souveniers, like the t-shirt featuring the Candy Bar Mascots! You'll find discounted merchandise (from previous seasons, usually) in shops located in both Rhineland and Tudor Square.

Leaving the park will be a breeze, if you've managed to park near Hershey Arena and Hershey Stadium—the exit lets you out right onto Hersheypark Drive, so you can start your weary journey to your hotel or home.

KENNYWOOD

4800 Kennywood Boulevard
West Mifflin, Pennsylvania 15122
412-461-0500
www.kennywood.com
Admission: $27 weekends; $22 weekdays
Operating Schedule: Late April through Labor Day. Park opens at noon, closing times vary.

Park History

This one-hundred-year-old park has been owned and operated by the same family since its opening. Major expansions came in the mid-1970s, and early 1990s, and the entire park is now a National Historic Landmark, considered one of the best "traditional" amusement parks in the world.

Major Attractions

Phantom's Revenge—Steel non-looping hyper coaster

Thunderbolt—Wooden ravine coaster

Noah's Ark—Classic walk-through funhouse

Racer —Wooden dual-track racing ravine coaster

Jackrabbit—Wooden ravine coaster

Getting There

Take I-376 to exit 7, Swissvale, and follow the yellow Kennywood arrows to the park. This can be a bit complicated, as you'll be driving through local streets, so make sure you keep your eyes open for the arrows. Once you've reached the bridge crossing the Monongahela River, the park will be to your left, and you'll be able to see the taller rides.

Planning to Go

Call the park for discount information. Coupons may be available throughout the Pittsburgh area. The admission price is a *great* bargain, however. You may want to ensure a weekday visit to the park, since the crowds will be smaller, and so will the admission price.

Beginning Your Day

The park has a general admission ticket that allows you into the park (with no rides) for about $5 and offers ticket books to pay as you go for individual rides. Unless you absolutely know you won't be going on more than one or two rides, opt instead for the pay-one-price admission, since Kennywood can be addictive and you just might find yourself doing more than you expected. The gates open about an hour before the rides do, so feel free to get to the

RAPIDS   KIDDIELAND   FERRIS WHEEL   FLUME

THUNDERBOLT

TURTLE   NOAH'S ARK   CAROUSEL   RACER

KANGAROO

PITTFALL   PHANTOM'S REVENGE   JACKRABBIT   OLD MILL

PITTSBURGH PLUNGE

EXTERMINATOR   MAIN ENTRANCE

WHIP   KENNYWOOD

park early; you'll be able to walk around and scope out the park. Situated on about forty acres, it's a smaller park that won't create tired legs, and even on weekends, you'll be able to do all you want and still have plenty of time left to do more.

In the Park

Kennywood's parking lot is multitiered, and unless you're lucky enough to have secured one of the street level spots, you might be parked on top of a huge hill. But don't fret, because you'll get to ride the sky ride that takes guests down the hill to the main entrance—which is, in itself, a great way to begin the day at the park.

At the main entrance, purchase your entrance ticket, and get a wristband at the entrance gate—which also contains metal detectors (no, the park isn't a nest of trouble makers, but this is how they keep it that way!). Expect to be searched, even if you don't set the metal detector beeping.

Once you pass through a tunnel under Kennywood Boulevard, you'll be in what many consider the finest traditional park in the country. The park contains many modern thrill rides, but also an abundance of classic rides you just don't see in any parks anymore, and all of them are meticulously maintained.

Since this isn't a theme park, there are no "defined" areas to group rides and such. It's perhaps best to make your way over to the huge steel Phantom's Revenge and make that your starting off point.

Back in 1990, the park made quite a controversial decision to add a huge, looping steel terrain coaster, which was quite contrary in nature to the rest of the park's offerings. Steel Phantom, as the ride was called, featured the fastest speed of any operating coaster at the time, a whopping eighty-nine mph. It achieved this speed by plummeting down the mountainside upon which the park rests, a breathtaking 225 feet! A full ten years later, the decision was made to replace the fast and furious coaster, but a public outcry convinced the park to leave the beginning of the ride (a 160-foot twisting first drop, and the second drop of 225 feet down the hillside) and just remove the loops that comprised the finale of the ride. Phantom's Revenge, as the new design was called, incorporated the best of Steel Phantom, and added new twists and hills, but without a single inversion element (the redesign also increased the second drop to 230 feet). This is obviously the single biggest thrill ride at the park, but be forwarned—it very rarely runs two trains, so it will have a long line from opening 'til closing. Get your rides in early, before the line builds up. In fact, take advantage of the park opening time (as opposed to the ride opening time) and queue up for Phantom before the rides even begin to operate. You won't want to wait on this line again for the rest of the day, although you'll be tempted.

You'll notice that you're in an area called "Lost Kennywood." (What did we say about this not being a theme park?) Yes, it's a themed area, added during the early 1990's to capitalize on the theme park nostalgia craze. All the buildings are inspired by long-closed amusement parks, and if you don't look too closely or touch anything, you'll feel that good old nostalgia for hours. If you *do* look closely, you'll find that many of the structures are made of fiberglass, and that gorgeous stone balustrade surrounding the reflecting pool is . . . is . . . *plastic*. The area then disappoints even further by containing a collection of rides that are totally out of place in this historic-looking area. Most are modern, flashy contraptions, and just don't belong. There's even a brand new older-style Loop-O-Plane (an early upside-down ride), which would be nicely placed if it weren't for the fact that the ride dates from the 1940s at the earliest, and this section is most definitely intended to be turn of the century. *Then*, there's the giant steel coaster towering over the entire area, and to add insult to injury, the 250-foot tall Pittfall, an ultra-modern freefall tower, anchors one end of the section.

Oh, well, on to the good stuff. Lost Kennywood also contains an honest to goodness classic Whip ride, and of these very rare devices, it's one of the best currently operating. The section also contains the Pittsburgh Plunge, a shoot-the-chutes that, while a modern ride, is disguised to look like an old-time classic, and actually succeeds in doing so. The twenty passenger boat splashes down in a huge reflecting pool, complete with fountains. The other great features of Lost Kennywood are the buildings that house gift shops and restaurants, which are all absolutely gorgeous and outlined in white, twinkling lights.

After exiting this themed area in "America's Finest Traditional Park," one finally begins to experience the essence of Kennywood. To the left is a Turtle (Tumble Bug for you classic ride fans), one of only three currently operating in the world. It consists of a train of turtle-shaped vehicles on a round, undulating track, and on each turtle is a passenger area featuring circular bench seating. Each turtle holds about six passengers, and when the ride begins to move up, down, and around, riders slide and bump into each other with abandon. More hilarious than thrilling to ride, it's an experience not to be missed. Next to it is Thunderbolt, a classic wooden roller coaster that is built on the side of a ravine. It has a large drop right out of the station, and a lift hill in the middle of the course, which carries the train to the highest point of the ride and enables this

Boating on a peaceful lake and coasting on a National Historic Landmark coaster, just two of the pleasures of Kennywood. (*Credit: Frank De Santis*)

crafty little coaster to finish with the two largest drops on the entire ride, eighty and ninety feet long.

Nearby is Noah's Ark. At one point, dozens of these rocking boat walk-through funhouses existed throughout the world. There are currently only two, and this is the only one in America. Completely rebuilt in the mid-1990s, this Noah's Ark has been modernized with some very clever illusions, and in answer to its popularity, extended in length. Don't miss it.

Heading to the other side of the park, you'll encounter the Racer. It's a dual-track racing wooden coaster . . . or is it? The train that starts on the left track actually returns to the right track at ride's end, and vice versa. This is one of the rare single track racers, with a continuous track—meaning one half of the ride is built following the course and profile of the other half, so that it appears there are two different tracks. It *always* confuses first-timers. The ride itself is family oriented, but with a few thrills along the way to provide some hoots and hollers. The Racer station was recently stripped down to reveal the original wooden lattice work, and it's truly beautiful.

Right next door is Jackrabbit, the smallest adult coaster in the park—but looks can be deceiving. Jackrabbit only features four drops. *All* of them are into a ravine, and drop #3, coming directly after the mid-course lift hill, is perhaps one of the great drops on a wooden coaster. It's a double dip, which means it levels off half way down, then plunges again. The effect of this in the rear of the train is ejector airtime, which always sends shocks of fright through riders.

The park contains a fabulous kiddie land, featuring many modern kids rides, as well as a few classics that parents might remember from their own early trips to parks.

As previously noted, Kennywood contains some very classic, rare rides—most notably, the Kangaroo, which is a "Flying Coaster" featuring long benches travelling in a circular motion at a high speed. At one point, the "track" features a ramp, which the bench flies up, over and off the edge of, producing a distinct bounce. This is pure nostalgia, as it might just be the only ride of its kind currently operating in a fixed site amusement park. There's also the Auto Ride, a *very* classic kiddie ride featuring electric powered cars that run in a wooden trough, and a speed a bit faster than you'd expect. The ride dates from the earlier part of the last century. You'll also find an old-fashioned dark ride at the park, a classic antique car ride, and an Old Mill—a boat ride through the dark with spooky scenery that proliferated at parks in the early 1900s. *All* of these rare rides are worth the price of admission unto themselves; they are the very reason to be at this particular park, as they just don't exist anywhere else.

Another reason to go to the park is the food. It's very classic amusement park fare, and it's all delicious (many guests claim to never have eaten a bad meal at Kennywood, and it's often voted as having the best park food). It's also very reasonably priced. The star food item at the park is probably the Potato Patch, a french fry stand that will make your mouth water with its incredible variety and quality. One reason *not* to be at the park: the entertainment. You've never seen a bigger bunch of untalented people in a show in your life—but if you enjoy the amusement of seeing bad acting and singing in bad shows, this might be nirvana for you.

A word of advice: Kennywood offers many ways to have a superb day at an amusement park. It's got a great collection of rides; it's got great food; the setting, landscaping and park architecture are wonderful; and it amounts to just about the most nostalgic amusement park experience there is. However, with all this good, there comes some bad, and it might just rub you the wrong way. Roller coasters will *never* open with multi-train operation, even if the park is crowded. They will delay the line to add more trains later in the day, which means that if you try to go on one when the park first opens, you might wait as long as you will in mid-afternoon, when the rides are running at full capacity. If you're riding single, you will probably be paired with a total stranger, even on rides that seat guests in close and uncomfortable positions. The park has a "soft" closing, which means it will stay open past the posted closing times, but ride operators will lower capacity on the rides to get people to leave. Because of this policy, you just never know just how you'll be ending your day at the park. The staff here can appear to be disinterested at best, and at worst, downright rude.

All that said, Kennywood is a great park, and if you can overlook the bad (all aspects of operation and management, really), then you just might leave thinking this is your all time favorite amusement park. It certainly is economical, and delivers the goods in abundance.

KNOEBELS AMUSEMENT RESORT

RR 487, PO Box 317
Elysburg, Pennsylvania 17824
1-800-487-4386
Admission: Basic pay-one-price: $22.75; pay-one-price with wood coaster
    option: $27.75; (both are available weekdays only—weekends are pay
    as you go)
Operating schedule: Late April through early October, 11 A.M. 'til 10 P.M.

Park History

A family-owned, traditional amusement park located in central Pennsylvania. The park prides itself on buying used rides, rehabilitating them to the point where they look brand new (referred to by fans as "Knoebelizing"), and offering a purely traditional, inexpensive, classic amusement park experience.

Major Attractions

Twister—Wooden roller coaster

Phoenix—Wooden roller coaster

Haunted House—Classic ride-through dark ride

Getting There

Take I-80 to exit 232, Buckhorn, and follow Rt. 42 south through Catawissa. Then, follow Rt. 487 (on your right) until you reach the park entrance on the left side of the road. These are rural roads, with not completely visible signs, so be very careful to watch out for them.

Planning to Go

This is perhaps the most inexpensive major amusement park in the country. Rides are frequently priced at $1 or less. Food, which can range from traditional park burgers and dogs to a full sit-down meal, can be had for less than half the price it costs to *park* at a major theme park. Call the park for any discounts that might be available (there are sometimes special two-for-one wristband days scheduled, or deals on ticket books).

Beginning Your Day

Knoebels is the epitome of the classic, traditional, family-owned-and-operated park. Members of the family live on the property; there is no entrance fee, nor is there a parking fee. Rides, food, and merchandise are all priced at the low end, and yet the park is not a "poor man's" version of an amusement park. All the rides are impeccably maintained and well-groomed. The park is beautiful, and it is located deep within a forest.

Get to the park early, and you might stand a chance of parking close in. The park has a huge parking lot in a flat field, and since it's so easy to enter and leave, you may want to have your car nearby. There is also a small lot located near the Phoenix roller coaster. You might try getting a space there, in which case you'll be parked practically in the park. It's a very laid-back atmosphere here; the layout has no rhyme or reason, and it's a great place to just stroll around.

The steep pay-one-price wristband (even steeper if you add the "wood coaster option") is, quite frankly, not worth it. It's only available Monday through Friday, under the logic that it would be too crowded on weekends to get your money's worth. Truth is, the park can be so crowded on weekdays, you may just not get a good value from it then, either. You'll want to do a *lot* in this park, but you'll also want to eat tons of the amazingly good and inexpensive food, and browse the shops, so you're not going to be just riding rides here. The park sells ticket books, and the highest price for a ride is $2 for the Twister roller coaster (not a typo, that's two dollars!!!), and before you think the major coasters aren't all that grand, note that both Twister and Phoenix appear on many top ten wooden coaster lists worldwide, including the one in this book.

Plan a leisurely day, come and go as you please, and you'll thoroughly enjoy yourself.

In the Park

If you're smart, you will arrive early enough to secure a parking spot in the Phoenix lot. Just in case you're in the main lot, but lucky

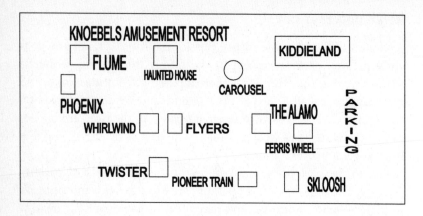

enough to be close in, we'll take our tour from the main parking lot end of the park. The layout is basically rectangular, but with no clear midways, so rides just magically appear right in front of you.

There is a former rural route, now closed, running along one side of the park. At the main parking lot end of the park, there are now rides right on this road (most of the park is unpaved gravel). The collection of carnival rides at this end of the park has newer-style spin machines, purchased brand new from the manufacturer (amazing for this particular park). The giant gondola ferris wheel, however, arrived used and was restored, and there are a few classics that have been in operation at the park for years and were originally located here (Whipper, Scooter Boats, Merry Mixer). Two of the favorites in this end of the park are the Bumper Cars, which are classic, well-maintained, and often voted the Best Bumper Cars in America, and the High Speed Thrill Coaster, which is kiddie coaster-sized, but operates in a manner that turns it into a bucking bronco.

Closer to the ferris wheel are modern contraptions known as Power Surge and Downdraft—one is a totally new-fangled ride, the other a newly designed ride based on a 1940s device. This area is also home to Sklooosh, a shoot-the-chutes named, according the the park's owner, for the sound today's chute rides make.

Knoebels' Twister during winter construction. (*Credit: Courtesy of Knoebels Amusement Resort*)

As you head down the former rural route, the Knoebels Swimming Pool is off to the left, and beyond it, one of the world's best wooden coasters. Twister, built in 1999, was patterned after a beloved classic in Denver, Colorado, at the old Elitch Gardens. It's a masterpiece of design, and a truly thrilling, rough and tumble ride.

It features some superbly designed drops, a huge double helix (hence its name), and great airtime and laterals. *Many* consider it only the second-best ride in the park!!!!!

To experience what top ten coaster lists all over the world say is the best ride in the park, one need only continue walking down the park road. At the end of it, is the Phoenix, a fantastic ride with a fantastic story.

Originally built in 1948 for San Antonio, Texas's Playland, the coaster was moved to Knoebels board by board in 1985, where it was rebuilt, restored, and renamed Phoenix. This classic figure-eight design features a relentless series of rabbit hops, all producing exquisite airtime, and is still the most beloved ride in the park. Its small size belies its thrilling nature, yet it's not inappropriate to bring all family members on for a spin. For sedate riding, a classic Antique Car ride cuts through the structure of Phoenix—it's a great, long ride, and very cool to have the Phoenix train roar past you as you're slowly cruising along in your turn-of-the-century vehicle.

The main water ride at this end of the park is a fantastic water flume with two solid drops, a tunnel, and terrific atmosphere.

Directly down the path from the Phoenix/Flume area, you'll find the center of the park, which contains a few classic rides that are not to be missed, as well as one of the park's showpieces. The park has a historic Flying Scooter ride (tubs on cables that offer riders the chance to steer giant fins and "fly" the tubs into the air). There's also a rocket ride, with levers to control the level the vehicles rise in the air, and Paratrooper, a legs-dangling, spinning, up-in-the-air-and-down ride. The real star of this area of the park, however, is the Haunted House. Built totally in-house by the park management staff, it's an innocuous looking little "house," which contains perhaps the best classic dark ride in the country. It's divided into "rooms," each containing so many stunts that one ride is not enough—you have to do it several times to catch all that's going on inside.

Leaving this area of the park, guests cross over one of the his-

torically landmarked covered bridges of the area, and arrive at the
Carousel. This classic ride is one of the few remaining to offer
riders the chance to catch the brass ring. It's a beautiful machine.
Nearby is the park's kiddie land, serving up dozens of new and old
kiddie rides, in the inimitable Knoebels style.

The amazing food services department at Knoebels works over-
time to ensure high quality at a low price. For proof of this, visit the
Alamo, a sit-down restaurant that always has a long line of diners
waiting to get in. Full course dinners can be had here for what
you'd pay for a burger and fries elsewhere, and the service is fast
and friendly. The food is also delicious! If you're in more of a hurry
to grab something, any of the dozens of food outlets in the park
will serve you well. Cesari's Pizza, located near the Haunted House,
is often voted the best park pizza in the country, while burgers, steak
sandwiches, hot dogs, and just about everything else you could possibly eat, are here and incredible.

The park is not strong on live entertainment, but frequently live
bands perform there. It's almost as if such entertainment would be
a bit *too* much—there's so much to do already.

If you like to shop, there are some charming non-park merchandise shops within the park, selling everything from Christmas items
to authentic German beer steins. Prices are decent, but there's also
a discount shop located near the water flume that sells merchandise
from past seasons.

You won't want to leave this park, as many who come here will
tell you. In fact, this is another park that will remain open past
posted closing times so that guests can get one more spin on their
favorite. If you *really* don't want to leave, though, book a campsite,
cabin, or cottage. They're located right in the park (some of the
cottages are literally right next to rides). They're not expensive, certainly more quaint than luxurious, but they book fast, so inquire
early in your planning. Then, you have the ability to sleep right in
the park, wake up the next day, and do it all over again.

SIX FLAGS GREAT ADVENTURE

PO Box 120—Route 537
Jackson, New Jersey 08527
732-928-1821
www.sixflags.com
Admission: $45.99 (theme park/safari park), $22.95 junior; $17.50 (safari only); $29.99 (Six Flags Hurricane Harbor); $59.99 (three park combo ticket)
Operating Schedule: Good Friday through Halloween. Opening generally 10 A.M., closing varies with season.

Getting There

Take the New Jersey Turnpike to exit 7A, and follow I-195 East to exit 16, Rt. 537. The park entrance is on your right.

Park History

Opened in 1974, this was a pretty-looking, but low on thrills theme park with very little "theme." Purchased by Six Flags in 1977, the park began an expansion that hasn't stopped yet. The recent addition of twenty-five new rides, along with several high-profile roller coasters, enabled the park to be listed in the 2003 edition of the Guinness Book of World Records as the park with the most rides (seventy-one) in the world. It is traditionally the park with the highest attendance of any seasonal park in America. A three park complex, it's the home to a theme park, a safari park, and a water park (all separate admissions).

Major Attractions

  Nitro—A 230-foot-tall non-looping steel hyper coaster
  Superman Ultimate Flight—The Northeast's first "flying" coaster, with passengers hanging in horizontal position below the track

Medusa—The world's first "floorless" looping steel coaster

Batman and Robin: The Chiller—Dual-track, linear induction motor launching shuttle loop coaster

Hurricane Harbor—The largest new water park in America

Wild Animal Safari Park—The world's largest drive-through safari outside of Africa

Planning To Go

A Six Flags season pass is essential to anyone who plans to visit more than one Six Flags park in a given season, or who plans to visit the same Six Flags park twice. A daily admission ticket price to any of the Six Flags parks is more than half the price of a season pass, plus season pass holders get a coupon book filled with additional goodies. Plus, a season pass enables the pass holder to purchase a season parking pass, usually for the cost of two or three visits. Even if you only use the season pass twice, it will save you money.

If you're dead set against the season pass, you can usually find $10 off coupons in fast food chains or supermarkets in the region in which the park is located. This park usually has a tie in with Burger King or McDonalds, both of which have resturants located just down the road from the main entrance, and each season has discounts on soft drink cans (Coca-Cola). Whatever you do, you don't want to pay full price to enter the park—no one does, so why should you?

If you decide to include Six Flags Hurricane Harbor in your visit, two days is a must. The park has a tropical theme, and it will make you feel completely transported to an island in the South Pacific. Offerings include a tremendous wave pool that is beautifully themed, various thrilling slides, an interactive play area, and one of the world's longest and most unique lazy rivers.

Beginning Your Day

Six Flags Great Adventure operates in just about any type of weather, unless there is extreme and prolonged thunder and/or lightning. This is a great park to visit in less than perfect weather, since it will be extremely uncrowded, and rides will operate. Try to avoid going to the park on any weekend, especially during the summer. It will be packed.

Plan to get to the park before 9 A.M. The adjacent Wild Safari Animal Park, a drive through, opens at 9 A.M., and if you don't dawdle, you can be through it and at the main entrance by 9:45 (the admission ticket to the safari is included in your theme park admission, so you might as well see it). The main entrance will not open 'til 10 A.M., unless it's an exceptionally crowded Saturday, so getting there early won't get you in the park early. If possible, have either your processed season pass or a pre-purchased admission ticket handy. Otherwise you'll have to wait on two slow-moving lines to purchase a ticket and gain access to the park. There are metal detectors at the main gate, so be prepared to be searched if the alarm goes off.

In the Park

Once you enter through the main gates, you're on Main Street, an area filled with shops that feature mostly Six Flags and park merchandise. If the park opens the gates a few minutes early, you'll be permitted to browse the shops, grab a refreshment, or head on down to the main entrance fountain, where, promptly at 10 A.M., a festive show featuring the Looney Tunes characters begins. At this point, security ropes also drop, and while others are watching Tweety sing and dance, head to the right toward Batman and Robin: The Chiller. It's hard to miss—its bright red and bright blue spikes tower 200 feet in the air (the ride is just past the Spinmeister and Music Express). While it's a dual-track coaster, it is only possible to

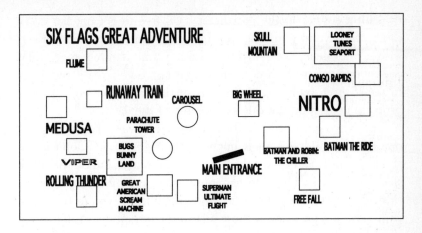

operate one train on each track (it's a forward and backward shuttle). *A long line on this ride can take forever, so you'll want to get on it first thing.* There's a hitch to this plan, however, since Chiller works by way of linear induction motors, which have yet to be foolproofed (meaning that sometimes they are troublesome). Therefore, Chiller might not always be open when the park opens. If it is, you'll have a few rides before huge crowds arrive. If It isn't, keep checking back periodically throughout the day—if you're lucky enough to catch it when it's just opening, you'll encounter the same small crowds as first thing in the morning. Chiller is the ultimate in thrill riding that features a 0-70 mph blast off into several inversions, a climb up a 200-foot-tall tower, and then a backwards plunge through the entire course. It's quite the wake up call.

After Chiller, it's a good idea to hit the other superhero ride in the Movietown section, this one simply called Batman The Ride (Robin wasn't involved in this one). This can be another slow-moving line, so you want as short a queue as possible. It's a four-across, inverted, outside looping machine. The ride is very intense, and might leave you a little disoriented.

You might be tempted to head on over to the giant blue, yellow, and pink coaster that towers over Batman The Ride. This is Nitro, the tallest coaster in the Northeast. Feel free to get on, but don't think you have to grab rides on this while you can get them. Even with a full queue, the Nitro line waiting time is rarely more than twenty minutes (with three trains operating). If you ride early, check to see if three trains are operating—if they are, you won't have a problem getting on the ride at any time of the day.

The Nitro queue is directly across from Looney Tunes Seaport, one of two children's areas in the park. Many guests don't know about this one, and crowd the older Bugs Bunny Land on the other side of the park. This one has more rides, and more importantly, rides that parents and kids can enjoy together. If you're travelling with kids, hop on a few of these hilarious contraptions. You'll enjoy it, and so will your kids!

If you're not travelling with kids, say a prayer that it's not too windy for the Sky Ride to be operating, and head directly for it. It will take you to the other end of the park, to Frontier Adventures, and you might just beat the majority of crowds to that end of the park as well. The entrance to the Sky Ride is located near the Big Wheel (a 150-foot ferris wheel), and it's one of the few remaining rides of its type in the country. It offers spectacular views, and allows riders to scope the lay of the land, as the location of every major ride and attraction within the park can be seen from its gondolas.

Disembarking the Sky Ride in Frontier Adventures, you'll find yourself in a giant fort structure. The park's Runaway Mine Train roller coaster is located here. It's normally a slow moving line, and was the park's first roller coaster (so it's a *very* tame but fun ride). If the line is already down to the bottom of the station's stairs, skip it. If not, hop on board, because it will bring you very close to your next objective: Medusa.

Medusa was the world's first "floorless" coaster. Built in 1999, it's a seven-inversion steel looping model, and from a distance looks rather "traditional" (if a giant looping roller coaster can be considered traditional). The ride vehicles, however, surprise new riders each and every time. The coach has been "stripped" of sides, fronts

Panorama of Six Flags Great Adventure, with Batman and Robin: The Chiller dominating the skyline. (*Credit: Paul De Santis*)

and floors, leaving what amounts to a chair attached to wheels that fly along the course. Passengers' legs dangle inches over the track, and from the front seat, the experience is nothing short of remarkable. You'll feel as if it's just you—no train, no riding buddies—flying over the track and through the convoluted course.

Exiting Medusa, head to the right, and over the foot bridge that leads to the Mexican-flavored section of Frontier Adventures. This is where you'll find Viper, a small, double-inversion steel coaster that features an inline heartline barrel roll as its penultimate moment—a moment where your vehicle revolves around your heart a full 180 degrees while it's moving forward. It's a fun but minor attraction that is frequently not available at all hours of the operating day.

Next door, however, is one of the park's most popular rides. Rolling Thunder is a dual-track wooden coaster, with differing profiles offering a unique experience. You may not be able to experience the ride to its fullest, however, as the park tends to only open one side, and very rarely, when both sides operate, do the trains leave the station together.

The park's original kiddie area, Bugs Bunny Land, is located adjacent to this section of Frontier Adventures. It has smaller versions of some of the park's adult rides, and is quite popular.

Now, head on over to the Boardwalk section, where the towering Great American Scream Machine resides. It's a 173-foot-tall seven-loop monster, with a patriotic color scheme of red, white, and blue. When it operates three trains, the line moves rapidly, and it's one of the more solid thrill rides in the park. Next to Scream Machine is Superman Ultimate Flight, a "flying" coaster with passengers in a horizontal position for the entire ride, hanging below and lying on top of the track, depending on the point in the circuit where the train happens to be. It's a brief but exciting coaster "gimmick" ride that offers a new way to fly.

Boardwalk also contains a motion simulator, The Right Stuff, which is fun for the entire family, but can be a chore to wait for if the line is too long. Nearby are the park's upcharge attractions—a go-kart track, a sky coaster (combining bungee jumping with a pendulum swing), and Eruption, a variation on a bungee ejector seat. Sometimes the park discounts these attractions—don't do them if they are full price, since you don't need to spend more money for rides—and you can get similar thrills on attractions already included in the admission.

Leaving this area, you'll find yourself back at the main entrance area. There's still plenty to do, but you might have noticed something unsettling. Many flat rides, and perhaps a few of the majors, weren't operating as you travelled around the park. Six Flags seems to have a very unusual policy in operating their parks. They do not staff all the rides in a given park at all hours of the day. While this might not affect the major, signature rides, the smaller flat rides will definitely be part of the policy. There's no reason to get frustrated— most rides will indeed be available at some point during the day, but not necessarily when you decide you want to ride them. This affliction is known as "staggered" ride openings. You'll get the big coasters right at park opening, but it might take you a while to ride the Tilt-A-Whirl. The theory here is that as more customers enter the park, the more crowded it gets, and the more employees start their shift to accommodate the ever-growing crowd. This might not seem to be the best policy for total guest satisfaction, but it's here to stay, and is becoming frequent in all park chains, not just Six Flags. The upside to this is that, if you catch a ride in the middle of the day that is just opening, it won't have had time to build a line, and will therefore be a walk-on.

As noted, Six Flags Great Adventure has more rides than any other park in the world, a total of seventy-one. That's a few dozen more than all four parks at Walt Disney World combined. There are literally dozens of spinning, moving devices, some of which exist at other parks, but a few that don't. Let's take a look at some of the more unique rides, as we travel around the park again.

Back at the main entrance, head right, and right again, into The Old Country section. Here, one of the park's best spinning rides lurks behind the bumper cars. The Pendulum is a swinging, spinning disc that starts out slow but builds to a frenzied climax. It's a huge, high-capacity ride that eats the line, so don't worry if there's a full queue; it will only take about ten minutes to get on if there is. Skip Spinmeister and Music Express; they operate on standard theme park mode, which means they deliver a little less oomph than at a more traditional amusement park.

Movietown is home to an early-generation Freefall ride, which is basically an elevator that is dropped down a shaft. This one is one of the smoothest operating of its kind. Movietown Water Effect is a standard chute water ride, and by no means is it a must. Raging Rapids, part of a gray area (is it in Looney Tunes Seaport or Movietown?), is a long and sometimes wet river rapids ride that can be fun, but can also leave you dry and disappointed. The Seaport is the newest kids' area at the park, and has some interesting new fangled kiddie rides, plus an interactive soft play area that kids can enjoy for hours. Adjacent to the Seaport is Skull Mountain, a family friendly roller coaster in the dark that manages to be quite thrilling for a coaster of its size (forty feet tall, in case you were wondering).

The Lakefront area contains a family roller coaster (outdoors this time), known as Blackbeard's Lost Treasure Train. This is a fun little ride, suitable for all ages. Fantasy Forest is home to one of the few giant ferris wheels that can be found in today's theme parks, as well as the park's classic, antique carousel. Also located in this area is Houdini's Great Escape, a motion illusion ride that is quite effective in convincing passengers that they're flying in 360-degree arcs. Jumpin' Jack Flash, near the carousel, is a one-of-a-kind spinning, up in the air and down, high-capacity ride, the only installation of such a device in the country.

Next, you'll be heading into Frontier Adventures, where the only ride worth noting is the Saw Mill Log Flume, one of the park's original 1974 attractions. It's not the wettest flume on record, but floating over the trees that dot the lakefront in this area is really rather peaceful, and will make you forget about the more rambunctious sections of the park.

Six Flags Great Adventure offers a variety of shows, which change from season to season. There's the Showcase Theatre in Movietown, which normally offers a musical variety show, and the talent on the stage is quite frequently dazzling! In the Lakefront Section, two waterfront venues offer different styles of entertainment. The Grandstand tends to have water-ski stunt shows, while Fort Independence offers a quite interesting sea animal educational "show." The Great Arena in Frontier Adventures features name entertainment, usually included in park admission (check the ever changing show schedule for the line up). Of course, the Looney Tunes Characters are ever present throughout the park, and they stage full shows at the park entrance throughout the day.

Now, food. It's expensive, almost prohibitively so. Lunch for two will run over $20, and at times, you won't be entirely happy with the quality. Pack a cooler, or bring one with you and pick up some sandwiches at the Wawa (a convenience store) on the way to the park entrance. Make sure you bring plenty to drink and a way to keep it cold, as a soft drink in the park will run about $4.50. The park allows tailgate parties in the parking lot (just stay out of the traffic lanes), and a group can eat for the price of what it would cost for two in the park. That said, if you *do* plan on eating in the park, the only choice is Best of the West, for several reasons. First, it's located within the structure of the Saw Mill Log Flume, and is completely cut off from the hustle and bustle of the rest of the park. Second, the entire building is surrounded by a patio, offering outdoor dining on a raised terrace overlooking the lagoon the flume surrounds. Third, the food offerings are actually quite good—from barbeque chicken to pork, to beef, from full dinners to sandwiches. And fourth (actually the most important point), this is the only park restaurant that offers free refills on soft drinks—yes, fill up to your heart's content, but don't take advantage and bring in bottles to fill without making a purchase. There *is* someone watching, and they will, at the very least, humiliate you in front of your children!

There are a tremendous number of shops within the park. Most offer any variety of different Looney Tunes character merchandise, including the Looney Tunes Shoppe near the main entrance. Ride souvenirs can be found near the rides themselves and in the Main Street Market, located next to the Looney Tunes Shoppe. Dozens of other shops are located within the park, but for discounted merchandise, you'll have to really *shop*. While there was once a shop containing only marked down items, now all the shops offer regular price (and sometimes pricey) items alongside the items priced to move. You just have to look around. One shop where you shouldn't expect to find any discounted items would be the Looney Tunes Shoppe, which is the largest and most popular store in the park.

As night falls on Six Flags, the crowds will thin out, but not tremendously so. This park attracts all types of guests, from families and teenagers to young and middle adults, and even the families will hang on 'til the bitter end. The unfortunate result is that there is *always* a traffic jam getting out of the parking lot, and the road to the main highway will be jammed. So . . .

. . . delay your exit. You can get in line right up to park closing for any ride, so plan on doing so. Save some shopping for closing time also, the stores at the main entrance will remain open 'til the last customer has left. If the park is offering fireworks the day of your visit, enjoy them (sometimes they begin just as the park is officially closing). Take a leisurely stroll to the car, and hope that the traffic is moving out of the park. If it isn't, you might try heading to the left of the parking lot instead of following the traffic to the right, and leave via the employee entrance/exit.

And one *more* word on the season pass: this park always leaves you wanting more. If you live even within a day's drive, you'll be back again before the season is out, and you'll be sorry if you didn't get the season pass the first time around. Especially enticing late in the season is the park's Halloween festival, Frightfest, which is hugely popular, and features a decorated park with special ghoulish shows and attractions.

SIX FLAGS NEW ENGLAND

Rt. 159, 1623 Main Street, PO Box 307
Agawam, Massachusetts 01001
413-786-9300
www.sixflags.com
Admission: $39.99 (adult); $19.99 (junior)
Operating Schedule: Late April through Halloween. Open 10 A.M.
   until 10 P.M.

Park History

A park has existed on this site since the beginning of the century, the most famous one being Riverside Park, which opened in 1940. At the end of the twentieth century, it was purchased by Premier Parks, a large corporate park operator, which subsequently purchased the Six Flags Theme Park chain. The park was branded Six Flags New England in 2000, and to date, heavy investments include major land expansion, a new water park, and multimillion dollar ride additions. The park is now home to Superman Ride of Steel, which many consider to be the world's #1 roller coaster.

Major Attractions

> Superman Ride of Steel—Giant, non-looping steel hyper coaster
>
> Batman—The Dark Knight—Floorless, looping coaster
>
> Cyclone—Wooden, twisting roller coaster
>
> Island Kingdom—Massive water park
>
> Scream—Three-track freefall tower

Getting There

Take I-91 to exit 47W, and get on Rt. 159 North. Follow this road to the park, which is on your right immediately after you cross the Massachusetts border.

Planning to Go

While this is a Six Flags park, it doesn't have the land or ride capacity one might expect from a park that carries the Six Flags name. Avoid the park on weekends. Crowd patterns are difficult to determine, but earlier in the day seems a better option than later. Island Kingdom, a fantastic water park included in the admission price, will occupy many guests during daylight hours, leaving rides with manageable lines 'til dusk, when it begins to empty out. A season pass is essential if you plan to visit this or any other Six Flags park more than once.

Beginning Your Day

Get to the park as early as you can. The parking lot on the park side of the road is on the smallish side, and will fill up quickly. Once the main lot is full, you'll be directed across the road to what is commonly known as the Siberia of theme park parking lots, and it's a long walk through the lot, across the pedestrian bridge, and into the park.

Since this is a Six Flags park, rides tend to have staggered openings. The rides immediately inside the main gate (Thunderbolt, Scream) open first, but also have low capacity. Pray that the Super Heroes section directly behind these rides also opens with the park, and that the main attraction in this section, Superman Ride of Steel, is ready to roll. You'll want to get on that first, and multiple times.

In the Park

This is *not* a huge park, and almost isn't worthy of the Six Flags name. However, the company is trying. New areas, new rides, and a somewhat new attitude can make the park quite an enjoyable experience.

As you enter through the main gate, the park's classic carousel is a beautiful site to behold. Because of its location right inside the gate, it rarely has a long line at any point of the day, so feel free to ride it when you choose to.

Stroll down Main Street directly to the main midway, which is the cross roads of the park, and runs its entire length. At this intersection is the classic 1940 Thunderbolt wooden roller coaster, a moderately sized thriller that packs a bit of a punch for its size. Its design was inspired by a coaster at the 1939 World's Fair in Flushing, New York. Next to it is Scream, an awesome 200-foot-tall trio of towers that features vehicles that launch passengers to its full height, bring them down bouncing, and haul them up to the top and thrust them down again. Note: both of these rides have lower capacity, so if the line is long, expect to wait a while. Additionally, if

SIX FLAGS NEW ENGLAND

MAIN ENTRANCE

CYCLONE

CAROUSEL

ISLAND KINGDOM
WATER PARK

BLIZZARD RIVER

FERRIS WHEEL

BATMAN—
THE DARK
KNIGHT

SCREAM   THUNDERBOLT

MIND ERASER

SUPERMAN
RIDE OF STEEL

you're a front seat or back seat rider, forget it on the Thunderbolt. There is a no choice of seat policy; you're cattle prodded into the next available stall, and if you try to deviate from this practice, you'll be told, rather rudely, where to go (hopefully to the place they want you to sit).

The ride that everyone comes to this park for is directly ahead, towering over the park. Superman Ride of Steel is a 221-foot-tall hyper coaster, frequently named the #1 roller coaster in the world (including in this book). It's a spectacular ride; it assaults the rider with relentless drops and twists with diabolical turns, and basically eats other coasters for breakfast. And it does this while being a smooth, easy to ride coaster as well. *The* roller coaster masterpiece of our generation.

Next door to Supie's entrance is Nightwing, a rather bizarre but unique ride in which passengers are spun and flipped upside down while lying on their stomachs. It takes forever to load, is uncomfortable at best, and is only worth a spin if it has no line whatsoever—when it will still take forever to get on.

Superman will keep calling you back, and thankfully, it's about midpoint in the park. However, you should head on out to the midway and trek over to the north end. Here, you'll find the

The world's #1 roller coaster, Superman Ride Of Steel, plummets another train of screamers down its 221-foot-tall first drop. (*Credit: Frank De Santis*)

Cyclone, a wooden coaster that at one time rivaled the best of them, but now has been tamed in certain sections by reprofiling the hills. Yet in other sections it is more violent than a coaster should be. It doesn't quite know what to make of itself, unfortunately, and was far better when everyone knew it was just a mean screamin' machine.

There are a few interesting attractions in this area besides the Cyclone—Blizzard River is a fun rapids ride, and Time Warp is a 360 degree looping ride that leaves passengers' legs dangling as it executes its spins. Flashback is a boomerang coaster that one need not ride here (it's a production model found in far too many other parks with significantly shorter lines). The Sky Ride, while short, is a cute antique of sorts whose former home was Coney Island. There's also a standard-sized chute ride for getting wet.

Just off the midway on one side is the Looney Tunes Movie Town kiddie park. Opposite that is the entrance to Crack Axle

Canyon, a small themed area that features Houdini's Great Escape, an illusion ride also found at Six Flags Great Adventure, and Tomahawk, also a ride at Six Flags Great Adventure, which features a huge spinning disk swinging in a pendulous motion.

Okay, you're passing Superman Ride of Steel again, so it's a good idea to hop on and remember why you came to this park in the first place, before you head on down to the south end of the park.

This area of the midway is known as Rockville, and it's a nice 1950s-themed area with a few rides, but mostly contains themed food stands. You won't spend much time here, and that's a shame, since it's one of the best looking areas in the park. What you will do is head right for the giant ferris wheel, Colossus, which is surrounded by the largest collection of rides in the park.

There's an outside-looping, suspended roller coaster known as Mind Eraser (a production model that can be found in a few other parks), and a few spinning rides that can easily be missed. The park's flume is located here (skip it if it has a long line; you won't even get splashed), as is the newest addition to the coaster line-up, Batman—The Dark Knight. This is a smaller version of the floorless looping coasters that have come about in the last few years and is, in fact, too small to be effective. There are a few other spinning devices located in this area as well. Adjacent is Tiny Timber Town, a small area designed for children.

The entrance to Island Kingdom is also located in this section of the park. It's a nicely themed water park, with a standard selection of water park attractions.

Food at the park is a mixed bag. The selection is quite varied, and the quality isn't bad, but the pricing is outrageous, especially considering that this was a small traditional park just a few years back and still isn't up to major theme park standards. Your best bet is to have a tailgate party, if you were lucky enough to get a parking spot in the main lot adjacent to the park. As at many theme parks, you cannot bring food into the park.

For shopping, most of the park's shops are located at or near the intersection of Main Street and the main midway, including the park's largest shop, Looney Tunes Emporium. You'll find some discounted merchandise in the Six Flags New England Emporium located directly across from Looney Tunes, and discontinued items in Martin Murphy's General Store, located in Crack Axle Canyon.

Leaving the park at closing time can be a hassle, since the road leading to the park is a two-lane local road, and it's not designed for heavy, confusing volumes of traffic. Try leaving earlier, or plan on staying on late and leisurely making your way out of the park. Just don't forget to ride Superman Ride of Steel several times before you go!

5

THE MIDWEST

CEDAR POINT
HOLIDAY WORLD
PARAMOUNT'S KINGS ISLAND
SIX FLAGS GREAT AMERICA
SIX FLAGS ST. LOUIS
SIX FLAGS WORLDS OF ADVENTURE
WORLDS OF FUN

CEDAR POINT

1 Cedar Point Drive
Sandusky, Ohio 44870
419-627-2350
www.cedarpoint.com
Admission: $42
Operating Schedule: Early May through Halloween

Park History

Opened in 1870, this is the second oldest park in America. However, while others of this age have stayed small and quaint, Cedar Point has developed into a huge, complete resort, boasting the largest number of rides and roller coasters of any amusement park in the area, along with several full service hotels, a marina, a beach, and restaurants. It is often named the world's best amusement park (and it doesn't take the term "amusement park" lightly—the park is *not* a theme park, although it is as grand and spectacular in its nature as any of today's large theme parks). Most of the park's roller coasters were able to boast they were the longest, tallest and fastest in the world at the time of their debut, and one, Top Thrill Dragster, is the current title holder.

Major Attractions

Top Thrill Dragster—The world's tallest, fastest roller coaster, a whopping 420-foot-tall, 120 mph thrill machine (first full circuit coaster in the world to top 400 feet).

Millennium Force—Steel non-looping giga-coaster (first full circuit coaster in the world to top 300 feet)

Magnum XL-200—Steel non-looping hyper coaster (first full circuit coaster in the world to top 200 feet)

Wicked Twister—Steel U-shaped inverted shuttle coaster

Raptor—Steel inverted coaster

Power Tower—300-foot-tall freefall tower

Mantis—Steel stand-up coaster

Getting There

Take the Ohio Turnpike to exit 118, and follow Route 250 north into Sandusky. Once in town, there are signs directing the circuitous route to the Cedar Point Causeway.

Planning to Go

There are two points during the season when Cedar Point is at its absolutely least crowded: at the very beginning—on weekdays during the park's first two weeks of business—and the very last week

before Labor Day, also on weekdays. School is still in session in Ohio during these periods, and the park can be enjoyed to the fullest with, quite frequently, no lines at all on all of its rides. Definitely try to visit during these times.

It is essential to call the park and order a copy of the *Cedar Point Getaway Guide*, a guidebook that offers all the information you'll need to have a spectacular vacation. It is filled with several pages of coupons for park admission, discounts on Cedar Point resorts (and many of the other hotels and motels in the Sandusky area). The *Getaway Guide* is published annually in very early spring, over a month before the park actually opens to the public.

If you're planning to go to this location several times, or visit any of the other parks within the Cedar Fair, LP family (ValleyFair, Shakopee, Minnesota; Dorney Park and Wildwater Kingdom, Allentown, Pennsylvania; Worlds of Fun, Kansas City, Missouri; Knott's Berry Farm, Buena Park, California; and Michigan's Adventure, Muskegon, Michigan), you may want to look into purchasing a season pass. Depending on the length of your stay, the season pass might be a better value than purchasing a multiple day ticket just to Cedar Point. Compare figures and decide what the best plan is for you.

If you can at all avoid visiting the park in the rain, do so. There are times when every major roller coaster will close at even the slightest bit of rain (even without lightning being present); and there are other times when everything runs, despite torrents of rain falling. This inconsistency could cause great dissappointment, since you can't count on an empty park with all rides open, as you can at other parks. Compounding this situation is the fact that, since Cedar Point is a resort, rain doesn't necessarily cut down on crowds, either. If people are there, they're going to be in the park.

Beginning Your Day

The quickest way to get into Cedar Point is the Cedar Point Causeway, which leads directly over Sandusky Bay into the parking lot. The signs for the park throughout Sandusky will lead you directly to the causeway, and to the parking lot (plan on an early arrival, at least by 8 A.M.). As you approach the parking lot toll booths, stay to the left, and enter using the resort toll booth. They will ask you where in the resort you're headed—tell them you will be going to the Sandcastle Suites restaurant, the Breakwater Café, for breakfast. They will give you a receipt for parking, and indeed, go have breakfast at the restaurant. It's not only a great way to begin the day at the park (the view is spectacular, and the food is good, especially the all-you-can-eat buffet), but you can also hand in your parking receipt and have the amount taken off your bill. After breakfast, head right into the parking lot next to the Gemini and Magnum XL-200. This is a smaller parking lot, and you'll be a lot closer to your car should you choose to visit it during your stay in the park. There is a park entrance right next to the Magnum coaster, and this gate will put you right in the back half of the park. You can actually beat guests using the main entrance to all the most popular rides in this half of the park.

In the Park

When you enter the park through the Magnum gate, you'll find a short midway to walk down, and you'll have three choices to make: to your left is Magnum XL-200, the world's first full circuit roller coaster to reach over 200 feet tall; to your right is Gemini, a wood-structured, steel-tracked racing coaster, and directly ahead, Cedar Point's newest thrill ride, Top Thrill Dragster, a 420-foot-tall monster that launches its sixteen passenger trains at a top speed of 120 m.p.h. into a 90 degree vertical climb, and is climaxed by a 90 degree vertical plunge that spirals 270 degrees on the way down. Since this is the new baby in town, hop on the line immediately—there's a good chance that the ride will begin operating well before the 10 A.M. ride opening time (at Cedar Point, you can enter the park beginning at 9 A.M., even though rides traditionally don't begin operating 'til 10 A.M.). Then, hop on over to Magnum, a legendary hard-

CEDAR POINT

MILLENNIUM FORCE

MANTIS

MEAN STREAK

BLUE STREAK

IRON DRAGON

RAPTOR

TOP THRILL DRAGSTER

CAROUSEL

POWER TOWER

GEMINI

MAIN ENTRANCE

KIDDIELAND

MAGNUM XL 200

SOAK CITY
CHALLENGE PARK
GATE
CHALLENGE PARK

WICKED TWISTER

SOAK CITY

core thrill ride. Crossing both of these off your list right at the beginning of the day will start you off with a terrific adrenaline rush.

After Magnum, head to Gemini. This racing coaster has one of the highest capacities of any coaster in the world, a whopping 3,000 people per hour, so it hardly ever has a long line. You'll be able to get rides at almost any time of the day without much of a wait.

Head right after you exit Gemini. Looming in front of you is Mean Streak, one of the world's largest wooden coasters. It's a short walk through the western-themed area in the park, Frontier Town, and this early in the day, it shouldn't have much of a line at all. For the smoothest possible ride, sit near the back of the train, in odd numbered seats only.

You've now ridden four of the park's most popular thrill rides and walked a bit, so it's time to take a slight breather. Hop on the Cedar Point Railroad, which has a station right next to the Mean Streak's loading station, and take it to the Main Midway stop. You'll have time to relax a bit before your next onslaught of thrills.

The Cedar Point Railroad station where you disembark is located right near two more of the park's big thrill attractions: Millennium Force and Mantis. During its opening season, Millennium Force used a simple ride reservation system to keep wait times down. If you visit on an uncrowded day, you may just be able to hop on board at your leisure. This was the first full-circuit roller coaster to top 300 feet tall, and it is a fast, speedy ride, that, despite its huge height, is quite suitable for most family members. This attraction's sprawling layout covers a great deal more area of the park than any other ride at the park, though it may not seem that way. The colorful Mantis is directly across the midway, and it's a stand-up coaster with four inversions, incredible speed, and a disorienting layout. Extreme thrills abound.

Leaving Mantis, walk towards the small steel coaster ahead on the right. This is Wildcat, a portable-style coaster that is loads of fun—but only ride it if there is a very short line. It has low capacity, and is not exactly the type of ride one expects to find at a major park. Directly across the midway from Wildcat, there is a very nice family ride, Iron Dragon. This is a suspended coaster, with cars swinging freely below the track as the train travels through the undulating course. Don't let the nature of the ride scare you off— this is a *great* family ride, with enough chills and spills to suit the thrillseekers, but not so much that you'll be terrorized.

Upon exiting Iron Dragon, head to the midway area that has the park's Sky Ride dangling over it. This is the Main Midway, which early on in the park's career was, in fact, the entire park! There are two major rides located here—the huge, green Raptor, an inverted roller coaster, and Blue Streak, a fun wooden coaster that is the park's oldest existing ride. Check the line for Raptor; it's usually the first ride that people coming in the main entrance hop on, and it keeps the line all day (the only way you'll beat this one is if you visit during the special weeks that the park is not particularly crowded). Walk under Raptor to gain access to Blue Streak, which has long lines mid-afternoon, but shouldn't be too bad earlier in the day.

Your next stop should be Wicked Twister, which is located on the Oceana Midway, nearest the shore of Lake Erie and the Cedar Point beach. Make sure you check the line—the ride is a shuttle, capable of running one train, and therefore might be a better bet to try just before the park closes.

If you've accomplished all this in a few hours, you've done most of the major thrill attractions. It's time to slow down and take another round, but this time beginning at the Main Entrance.

One of the park's gorgeous antique carousels is located just inside the main entrance. Sadly, this beautiful ride is often bypassed by eager guests rushing to the bigger thrills further inside the park, so it rarely has any type of line. Enjoy a leisurely spin on it while you're in the neighborhood. The classic Sky Ride has a station located immediately behind the carousel, but pass on it for now, and keep strolling down the impressive main midway, as another rare, classic ride is just ahead.

Cedar Downs, located on the left of the main midway just past the cut through to Blue Streak, is a quite historic device, one of only three in the entire world. It may look like a carousel, but it revolves faster, and the horses lurch back and forth, as if they are actually racing each other around the circular course. It's part of amusement park history, and it should not be missed.

In the Blue Streak area are the Calypso, a spinning ride from the 1960s that's also a bit of a classic in this day and age, and a long and fun you-drive-them car ride themed to racing dragsters. Both rides can be passed up if they have lines, but they are fun to experience.

When leaving the Blue Streak area, cross directly over the main midway and head toward the tall spindle of a tower. It's a simple observation tower, and though it has spectacular views, it's not a must-ride. Next to it is Disaster Transport, an in-the-dark, outer space-themed roller coaster that is very suitable for the entire family, and is actually quite fun. The Giant Wheel, a 150-foot-tall ferris wheel, also provides spectacular views, but it is not one of the park's must-rides. Do it if it doesn't have any line at all.

You'll notice that you've circumnavigated the park's kiddie land, which is huge and delightful, with dozens of smaller versions of the park's adult rides. If you're traveling with children, this is a great time to stop and let them play in their very own area. If you have older kids whom you'd rather not have wandering around the park without supervision, they'll have a blast in the adjacent Coliseum, the huge, landmark ballroom at the park, which houses a massive arcade on its ground floor.

The selection of spinning rides you'll encounter as you make your way further into the park are typical—every park has them. Don't waste your time. You have bigger fish to fry, and the tall, four-poster tower that is just ahead and calling your name is one of them. Power Tower, the 300-foot-tall attraction featuring two different ways to scream, is one of the world's tallest thrill rides. When you enter the queue line, you'll eventually have to choose between the two thrills offered: on one, you launch from ground level all the way to the top at a fast speed, plummet back down, and bounce to a landing. On the other, you're taken up slowly all the way to the top, held there for what seems to be an eternity, and then launched down to the ground, where you bounce to your landing just like the first. Power Tower features two towers devoted to each type of program, but be careful that you choose the correct line when the queue splits. You're more than likely going to want to ride both sides. Continuing down the midway, you'll find Corkscrew, the world's first coaster to feature three inversions. It's primitive compared to today's mega-monsters, so don't wait on any type of line for it.

Further along the midway, past Magnum and Gemini, find your way back to Frontier Town. This western area contains shops, restaurants, and, most importantly, three of the park's water rides. Snake River Falls, one of the world's tallest water chute rides, is guaranteed to get you soaked, as is Thunder Canyon, a river rapids ride. For more of a splash than a total soaking, White Water Landing is a typical but fun flume ride. Also located here is Mine Ride, a family roller coaster with a bit of a punch. You might also want to check out the Cedar Point Town Hall, a museum featuring the illustrious history of the park, complete with photographs, antique souvenir exhibits, and classic arcade games. It's a nice place to cool off and catch your breath.

Towers and twirlers greet guests of Cedar Point. (*Credit: Frank De Santis*)

Now make a left out of Frontier Town, and follow Frontier Trail. Until the debut of Millennium Force, this was the most tranquil place in the park. A gallery of craft shops, craft demonstrations, animal farms, and just beautiful shaded peace and quiet, the Trail connects Frontier Town back to the Main Midway. You won't feel at all that you're in a huge amusement park, and you might just want to spend hours here.

Eating and entertainment in the park are in abundance. There are dozens of food stands and a few high quality, sit down, full service restaurants. Food pricing in the park is not that bad. On the Main Midway, there's an all-you-can-eat buffet (great for hearty appetites), which is an especially nice bargain. Several of the restaurants have live entertainment, and there are also theatres that specialize in high quality shows with extremely talented performers.

As dusk falls, several rides require a revisit. Millennium Force, Magnum XL-200, Raptor, and Mean Streak are all great night rides. Guests may enter the lines for any Cedar Point line right up to posted park closing time, so if there was something that had too long a line during the day, go ride it in the last minute the park is open.

If you haven't had your fill, there's still more to do. Since you have to exit the park through the Magnum gate, you'll be right in front of Challenge Park, on the peninsula next to your parking lot. Here, there are two different mini golf courses, a great go-kart track, a sky coaster, and a few other neat extra charge attractions. Challenge Park is open past the amusement park's closing time, and it's a great way to end the day. It's also less crowded here at closing time then it would be if you took time out from the day at the amusement park.

The nicest thing about ending your day at Challenge Park is that, when you prepare to leave the peninsula and head for the causeway, the main parking lot will have mostly emptied out, and you won't encounter any traffic heading back to the mainland and your hotel or home. Be sure to look in your rear view mirror—the entire park's roster of roller coasters remain lit up. It's an awesome image to behold.

HOLIDAY WORLD

PO Box 179
Santa Claus, Indiana 47579
1-877-463-2645
www.holidayworld.com
Admission: $28
Operating Schedule: May through mid-October

Park History

Holiday World debuted as Santa Claus Land in the mid-1940s with several attractions, shops, and—most importantly—a place to visit Santa Claus in the heat of the summer. The park expanded in 1984 to include new holiday sections geared toward Halloween and the 4th of July, and simultaneously got its new name. After the addition of a water park and several signature attractions, the park can now be considered one of the best family entertainment venues in North America. It annually receives awards for being the cleanest park in the USA, and is considered to have the friendliest staff. Having opened a full nine years before Disneyland, the park bills itself as America's First Theme Park.

Major Attractions

Raven—Wooden terrain roller coaster
Legend—Wooden terrain roller coaster
Splashin' Safari—Full service water park

Getting There

Take I-64 to exit 63, and drive south on Rt. 162 for seven miles, where you'll make a right turn at the "T" intersection. The parking lot will be on your right as you head up the hill.

Planning to Go

The park is least crowded during weekdays early in the season. The catch to this is that the park also closes earlier in the day at this time. Since both the Legend and Raven roller coasters are magnificent night rides, you might want to plan your trip for later in the season to accommodate for this.

Beginning Your Day

Upon entering the Holiday World parking lot, you'll notice one thing that's different from almost all other parks right away: there is no parking fee. Holiday World is one of the last remaining major parks in the country to offer this perk, and there is no doubt that it makes guests feel, right at the beginning of the day, that the park is there for them to enjoy, not to fleece every dollar out of their pockets. Obviously, the park scores high points for this first nicety.

The second thing guests will notice right away is the amazingly friendly employees. Many of the employees working in the park are members of the owner's family, and even those who aren't go far, far out of their way to make visitors feel right at home. As mentioned earlier, the park annually wins awards as having the best and friendliest staff of any park in the country.

In the Park

Once inside the main gate, you'll find yourself in the original themed section of the park, Christmas. The area is filled with Christmas-oriented shops and restaurants, and there are kiddie rides to your left. Make your way through Christmas, and just past the kiddie rides, you'll see the sign luring you into the Halloween section of the park and your first main conquest: Raven, a wooden roller coaster that has been named the world's number one wooden coaster on one recent list.

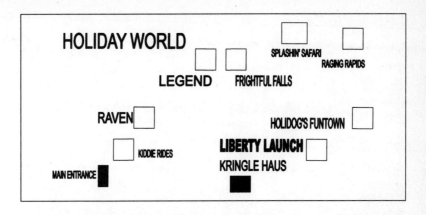

Raven, built in 1995, is a brief, but frantic experience. When it was built, it pushed the envelope for what a ride in a truly family park could be. It's a terrain ride (meaning that it follows the natural contours of the land that it's built on), and a combination of out-and-back and twister. With its ten-story height differential, it's no slouch in the thrills department, either. The ride begins with a fine first drop into a tunnel, and follows this with enough direction changes to disorient even the most seasoned rider. Then, just when you think things are beginning to calm down a little, Raven throws you for a loop by having a sixty-foot mid-ride drop into a valley, where it hugs the ground, dodges trees, and has a ferocious fan turn, before returning to the Victorian-themed building that houses the station. The ride *always* leaves all riders breathless, yet is not intimidating enough to ward off family members. It's just what a wooden coaster should be.

When leaving Raven, head on down the hill to your left for the next stellar attraction: Legend, another wooden roller coaster, takes all the thrills of Raven and triples them. Legend is also a terrain wooden coaster that combines out-and-back and twister elements. It's longer, taller, and faster than its older brother, and in fact, many consider it a better ride. This baby features a twisting first drop into a tunnel, followed by a mad race over airtime-producing speed hills,

Splashin' Safari's fantastic Zoombabwe water slide. (*Credit: Holiday World and Splashin' Safari*)

wicked turns, more speed hills, a second tunnel, and an awesome helix. Both coasters feature relentless pacing, which just adds to the thrills, and they give the park one of the best one-two punches in the business. People travel from all over the world to ride these two instant classic roller coasters.

At this point in the day, you may want to head into the Splashin'
Safari water park to cool off, and get your fill of water park rides.
The water park offers the standard collection of attractions: a wave
pool, lazy river, and slides (from mild to wild, including several that
are totally enclosed and in the dark). You'll have beaten the crowds,
and you can be done with the water park before midday, when, on
warm weather days, the water park is at its most crowded.

Plan on leaving Splashin' Safari after lunchtime. You can then
explore the rest of the park at your leisure, first stopping in the one
section of the theme park you missed on your way in during the
morning hours: the 4th of July. This patriotically-themed area houses
rides tied in to our American heritage, as well as eighteenth and nine-
teenth century historic Americana. And yes, the park offers a few
nods to its Indiana location as well. The area also contains most of
the park's flat ride selection, and is home to Liberty Launch, a towering freefall-style ride that both rockets and plummets passengers by
way of compressed air pressure. The very back of this section gives
way to a children's land devoted to Holidog, the park's festive mascot.

Once you complete a full loop of the park, you've seen it all, so
now you can slow down to smell the roses. You're now back in the
Christmas section, where Santa himself holds court each and every
operating day in the Kringle Haus. Try the pizza in Kringle's Café,
often noted as having the best pizza offered in an amusement park.
This section is also home to the Holiday Theatre. Rudolph's Rein-
deer Ranch, close to the main gate, is home to the park's kiddie
rides. Nearly a dozen shops fill the area as well, from park souvenir
items to hand-crafted gift items. Since most people will be further
into the park at this time, you'll be able to shop and browse at a
nice, steady pace without feeling too crowded in.

If you haven't noticed already, the park offers something that
should, in itself, give reason to be a frequent guest—free, unlimited
soft drinks, all day, every day. For a thirsty family accustomed to
paying up to $4.50 per drink at a major corporate theme park, this
extremely generous offer is sure to make a huge difference in the
budget planning.

Head back into Halloween. There are a few rides here you should check out. If you haven't gotten your fill of water park rides, there's Frightful Falls, a nice, family-style log flume. It's located at the base of the hill, adjacent to Legend. There's also a Scrambler, which is always a family favorite, and the Hallowswings, a swinging chair ride with festive Halloween theming. Of course, feel free to hop on board the Raven and Legend again and again, although you'll definitely want to experience both in the darker hours of the evening.

Following the midway again, you'll soon be back in the 4th of July section, home to Raging Rapids in Boulder Canyon, a river rapids ride also suitable for the family, although you'll get soaked. If you don't mind remaining a little damp, ride this late in the day, as more practical people want to be dry for the trip home, which means they probably rode it when the line was at its longest, at midday. Next door is a petting zoo, and nearby, in Holidog's Funtown, is the park's third roller coaster, Howler, which is essentially a kiddie coaster all family members can ride together. (All the attractions in Holidog's Funtown are designed to accommodate parents and children together, by the way!)

Make your way down the midway through 4th of July back to Christmas, pacing yourself as you go to allow time to sneak back into Halloween and get those night rides on the Raven and Legend. If you've timed it just right, you'll have time to wait on both lines before the park closes for the night, and you'll get to see just why both of these roller coasters are so revered. They are awesome by daylight, but at night, they become two totally different animals, and you won't soon forget them.

You'll have a few minutes to pick up last minute items in the gift shops located near the park's main gate, so stroll out at your leisure, and don't forget to grab one more cup of soda before you leave. And the very last thing you should do is make sure you tell the park staff just how much their free beverage service and free parking mean to you.

PARAMOUNT'S KINGS ISLAND

6300 Kings Island Drive
Kings Mills, Ohio 45034
1-800-288-0808
513-754-5700
www.pki.com
Admission: $42.99
Operating Schedule: Early April through Halloween

Park History

Taft Broadcasting, owners of an older Cincinnati amusement park known as Coney Island, built this grand theme park north of town in 1972. They moved most of the rides from the older park to here, recreating the main midway of the older fun spot as a new themed area that was just one part of a much bigger picture. Eventually, the park became the flagship of a major theme park chain, Kings Entertainment Company, which also owned and operated four other giant theme parks in North America. The parks were eventually purchased by Paramount, who rethemed them and added many movie-based rides and attractions, as well as branding them as Paramount Parks. They are now owned by multimedia giant Viacom, which counts Paramount Pictures among its many holdings.

Major Attractions

Beast—World's longest wooden roller coaster

Son of Beast—World's tallest, fastest, and only looping wooden roller coaster

Flight of Fear—Linear induction motor launching, indoor steel looping roller coaster

Top Gun—Movie-themed suspended steel coaster

Tomb Raider—Movie-themed indoor thrill ride with special effects

Getting There

The park is located just off I-71, 24 miles north of Cincinnati, Ohio. It is clearly visible from the interstate.

Planning to Go

If you plan on visiting other Paramount Parks in North America (Paramount's Kings Dominion, Doswell, Virginia; Paramount's Carowinds, Charlotte, North Carolina; Paramount's Great America, Santa Clara, California; Paramount Canada's Wonderland, Vaughn, Ontario), it would be wise to purchase a season pass. If not, the park offers discounts on tickets purchased in advance online. You must purchase your online tickets far enough in advance that they will be processed and either mailed to you or held at the main gate in time for your arrival, and you'll get $6 off the regular ticket price by doing so.

The park is least crowded at the very beginning of the season on weekends, during the week in its first few weeks of daily operation, or during the week in August before Labor Day, after which time the schedule goes back to weekend operations. The park is generally closed to the public for company buyouts during weekends in September.

Beginning Your Day

Taking either of the two exits off I-71 that lead to Kings Island Drive will position you right on the road dividing the parking lot from the interstate. For the best parking location, try using the north entrance to the parking lot, which will put you in the left section of the lot (when facing the park). You can usually park closer to the main outer promenade by using this side of the lot (there is also a preferred parking section, which has an upcharge) and it's usually a bit easier to get out of the lot at the end of the day using this area also. You'll probably want to exit the park a few times during the

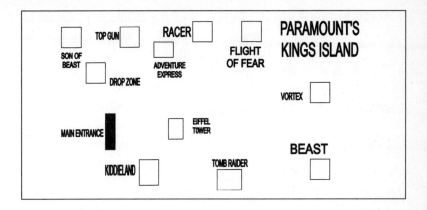

day, so get to the lot early (the park opens at 10 A.M.), to ensure the closest possible parking.

Stroll up the slightly inclined outer mall area to the main gate, where there are ticket booths ahead. Directly behind them are the main gate turnstiles, where you'll hand in your tickets and enter the park. Be prepared to have your breath taken away!

In the Park

As you enter through the turnstiles, you'll be in a covered area (the building above used to house a restaurant), so your view of the park will be slightly obscured, which is all part of the plan. Emerging into the park, and daylight, guests are confronted with perhaps one of the grandest entrances to any theme park, anywhere. Directly ahead is the International Street Fountain, a huge rectangle of dancing waters. Directly behind that is the park's landmark observation tower, a one-third scale replica of the Eiffel Tower. This is without a doubt one of the most impressive park entrances to behold, and it's won awards for just that.

International Street, which you're now at the foot of, is a themed area filled with shops and restaurants, offering both park souvenirs and hand-crafted gift items. But more on this spectacular section later.

Head directly down the right side of the fountain. Once at the Eiffel Tower, simply pass it and continue down the midway, past the theatre on your right, and head into River Town. You'll soon see a trail of footprints on the ground, which lead you directly to the entrance of Beast, the world's longest wooden roller coaster.

Beast is a terrain ride, hugging the ground during most of its course, which travels over the rolling hillsides of southern Ohio. It begins with a 135-foot drop into an underground tunnel, and from there feels like a runaway train. Riders always are surprised by the ride's second lift hill, which brings the train back up to a 141-foot height, and the ride's finale, a huge, 540 degree tunneled helix. Enjoy this ride a few times before the line builds up, as you won't be back to ride it again until much later in the evening.

Leaving Beast, turn right, and head towards the huge looping roller coaster next door, Vortex. This is a ferocious ride, and you'll probably only want to do it once, so enjoy it now while the lines are still very short. You're now on Coney Mall, the section of the park dedicated to the old Coney Island (which closed when Kings Island opened, but ironically has reopened and is going strong). Lining the festive mall are the park's major games, and along one side, the Racer roller coaster. This twin track beauty might be familiar as the ride that both the Brady Bunch and Partridge Family rode (although not at the same time). Vortex is at the far end of Racer, away from its station, but head on down the mall on the left side— before you race, you must take a Flight of Fear!

Flight of Fear is located behind Racer—the entrance to the ride cuts right through the structure. This is an indoor looping coaster that launches from 0 to 70 mph in about four seconds. Its tight, twisting layout is impossible to follow, and the ride is experienced with simple lap bars holding passengers in place.

Now, Racer. You'll notice that nowadays, you can ride in a very different manner than the Bradys or Partridges got to experience, as one side of the ride offers trains facing backwards. This is a very classic ride experience, no matter which direction you're facing, and

Get looped at Paramount's Kings Island. (*Credit: Frank De Santis*)

the ride was responsible for the resurgence of giant roller coasters built at theme parks in the 1970s.

Head away from Racer, and in the general direction of the natural wood roller coaster near the front of the park. This is Son of Beast, and it's in the Action Zone section of the park, where a few intense thrills await.

Provided that lines aren't too horrendous, try Face Off, first. This ride will probably have the park's longest wait time, since it's a shuttle and only can run one train. It's very similar in design to the overprolific Boomerang coasters (which are not recommended in any way unless they have no line—you'll find one eventually in your travels, so no need to waste two hours to ride one), but with a twist—the vehicles hang below the track, and, by facing even-numbered cars backwards, offers riders a chance to look directly at the faces of friends, strangers, or anyone else who happens to be sitting opposite. This can be a fun experience, but *don't* wait for it if the line is too long. Check for signs outside the ride, or ask an attendant.

Nearby is Drop Zone, one of the world's tallest freefall rides. This high capacity tower revolves slowly as it heads to the top of the 330-foot tower, then stops, holds there for a breathtaking few seconds, and plummets back to earth. Again, check to make sure the line isn't going to eat up hours in the park—this is a good thrill ride, but not worth missing others for. Top Gun, the park's suspended coaster, is also here, and it's a good ride either day or night. If the line for it extends under the tunnel, it's going to be a long wait, but you'll be more satisfied by this ride after a long wait than you would by Face Off or Drop Zone.

And now it's time for Son of Beast. This is the world's tallest wooden roller coaster (218 feet), the fastest (78 mph), and the only one to feature a 360 degree upside-down loop. Be prepared to wait a long time for it. Also be aware that the ride sometimes ceases operation in the middle of the operating day, may not open at park opening, and sometimes closes earlier than park closing (it is, after all, a *big* machine that needs constant care and attention). Also note that each of the three seat cars that are linked together to form a full train on the ride offer the best possible ride in the center seat (the smoothest ride always seems to be in the center seat of the very last car on the train). After you've been looped, head back to the main entrance.

If you're travelling with smaller children, Paramount's Kings Island will be their favorite park. Slightly down International Street on the right is the entrance to the park's huge children's section. There is both Hanna-Barbera Land, themed to the cartoon characters created by those famed animators, and Nickelodeon Central, offering wet, wild adventures. The areas are adjacent, and are crammed with enough to do to fill a day all by themselves. Major attractions include a Scooby Doo-themed dark ride, Scooby's Ghoster Coaster (a suspended roller coaster for families); The

Beastie, a wild junior wooden coaster; Nickelodeon's Splat City (use your imagination, and you'll be right on the money—be prepared to get wet); Runaway Reptar (another kids' suspended coaster); and just about every other type of ride and attraction geared towards children and their parents.

Just past the amazing children's section is the beginning of River Town (you've already seen the end of it, where the Beast lurks). Along this shaded, peaceful section of the park are the major water rides (a flume and a river rapids), plus Tomb Raider. This indoor, heavily themed attraction is a flip-you-upside-down high capacity thrill ride (commonly known as the Top Spin). This installation offers special effects galore, along with actual set pieces used in the Paramount production of *Tomb Raider*.

The entrance to Waterworks, the park's thirty acre water park, is also located in River Town, but unless you've planned two days at the park, you'll have to skip it. There just isn't enough time.

As dusk settles on the park, there's still a lot to do. There are several rides in the park you just don't want to miss a night ride on: Beast, your first encounter in the morning; Son of Beast (if the line isn't too long); Top Gun, the suspended coaster; and two new rides that you probably just breezed past earlier in the day. Adventure Express, a mine train roller coaster located near the entrance to Racer, will place you directly in an Indiana Jones movie; it's a fun, family friendly ride with enough thrills for all. The Eiffel Tower provides breathtaking views of the park and surrounding area, all accentuated at night by gorgeous lighting. From here, notice that the glorious international fountain is now ablaze in bright, alternating shades of colored light.

Back on International Street, grab some of LaRosa's Pizza (a famous Cincinnati institution, and often voted best park pizza by industry trade papers), and sit and relax after your marathon journey around one of the nation's best theme parks. You'll enjoy listening to the music playing over the speakers lining the midway, watching the fountain change patterns and colors, and knowing you've just completed a day at an awesome theme park.

The shops and restaurants on International Street remain open well past closing time, which is when you should be browsing, using the time to remain in the park and enjoy the atmosphere. The parking lot can be gruesome to escape when the park is crowded, so just hang out, relax, and wait 'til the crowds subside, and you'll be able to get right in your car and head onto Kings Island Drive, and your journey home.

SIX FLAGS GREAT AMERICA

542 N. Route 21
Gurnee, Illinois 60031
847-249-4636
www.sixflags.com
Admission: $40
Operating Schedule: Early May through Halloween

Park History

The park opened in 1976 as Marriott's Great America, one of three planned identical theme parks (the other two are in Santa Clara, California, and Washington, DC). Marriott quickly abandoned its plans to get into the theme park business, and this park was purchased by the Six Flags chain, with the California property going to Kings Entertainment (now Paramount Parks). The Washington, DC property was never built.

Major Attractions

Superman Ultimate Flight—Steel flying coaster
Raging Bull—Steel non-inverting hyper-coaster
American Eagle—Huge, twin-track racing wooden coaster
Batman The Ride—Steel, inverted outside-looping coaster
Viper—Wooden twister inspired by the Coney Island Cyclone

Getting There

The park is located just off I-94, Grand Avenue exit, in the town of Gurnee, and is visible from the highway.

Planning to Go

While the usual coupons are available (call the park to find out exactly which ones are in effect at the time of your visit), since this is a Six Flags Park, a season pass is recommended to get the best value throughout the summer, throughout the country.

The park can be quite crowded, and has an awkward layout (more on that later), so only plan to visit early in the season on weekends (Sunday is better), or early in the week during daily operations. Frightfest, held annually during the month of October, can actually be the most crowded time of the season.

Beginning Your Day

This is a Six Flags park. This means, unfortunately, that there will be times, even at the height of the season, that rides are not operational, or have staggered operating hours. Even a visit on a very uncrowded day does not guarantee the guest a positive experience, since that's when the park tends to cut back on staffing and operations (which means that many rides won't be open, and those that are will run at less than full capacity). It's almost better to visit this park during full season, on a weekday, to stand a chance of hitting all the rides you want to experience, at least at some time during the day.

In the Park

Remember the awkward layout referred to earlier? The designers of the park back in the mid-1970s wanted to try something new in theme park design, and this was the park where they tried it. Instead of a typical park layout, with many midways and "cross-streets", or the "hub" system that the Disney parks are patterned on, the two

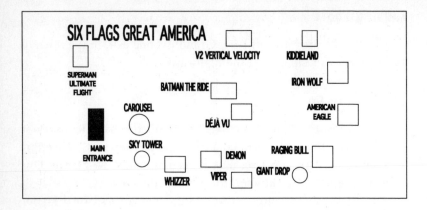

Marriott Parks were designed roughly in the shape of a donut. Once you enter, you either go left or right, and just follow the circular midway around until you arrive back at the entrance. In this way, the designers thought, one wouldn't miss any attractions, could easily just go from one to the next, and since half the people entering would go left, and the other half would go right, would tend to create a nice traffic flow in all areas of the park.

It didn't work.

Guests found that they didn't like being corralled and herded quite this way. They might just want to ride something twice. Perhaps after ride A, they might want to experience ride W, which was not the next ride in line. Funny, people have minds of their own.

Unfortunately, it was too late to do anything about the layout of the park, so it remains until this day, and it causes an awful lot of wasted time walking back and forth. It can be frustrating as well, as you might be standing right next to a ride that has its entrance exactly 180 degrees around from where you're standing. Six Flags tried to remedy the situation the best they could by adding an entirely new section to the park, which is the only area in the park that isn't part of the main "donut." It offers two entrances, adding the ability to walk through and keep flowing in one direction.

Oh, well. In spite of all that, this is a good park. It has some great rides, and the only way you'll be able to get on them all is to go around the park in a whirlwind at least three times before you slow down. So, tie up those sneaker laces, because here we go!

When you enter the park, you'll be face to face with the Columbia, a gorgeous double-decker carousel. Head left inside the entrance, and right over to the park's newest thrill ride, Superman Ultimate Flight.

This is a flying coaster, in which riders are tilted forward until they face the station's floor in a true flying position. The ride zooms through inversions while both dangling riders in this precarious manner and also flipping them onto their backs to enjoy a sky high view. Because of the new fangled design of the vehicles, loading will probably take a while, so be prepared.

Continue in the same direction, left of the carousel, and you'll come to Batman The Ride and V2 Vertical Velocity. V2 is a shuttle and only operates one train, so ride it now, as the line could reach unmanageable proportions later in the day. Bypass Batman The Ride for now. Keep heading towards the back of the park, as just behind Batman The Ride is Déjà Vu, another shuttle looping coaster with only one train. Because of the layout, you'll have to walk entirely around the park to reach it. *Make sure* you see it running before you venture to it, as it has a tendency not to be operating. If it isn't, feel free to hop right on Batman The Ride, as it's one of the lower capacity rides in the park as well.

If you're lucky enough to have gotten on Déjà Vu, you'll now be on the side of the park that was to the right of the carousel, and you've just ridden the three rides in the park that have the lowest capacity. (If you decided to do Batman The Ride as well, then that makes the four rides with the lowest capacity.) In any event, head directly into the Southwest Territory for the two best coaster experiences in the park. Raging Bull is a steel coaster topping out over 200 feet in the air, with a smooth as silk ride on a twisting layout. Viper, right next door (but a rather long, awkward walk) is a wooden coaster patterned after the Coney Island Cyclone. It doesn't have the intensity of that ride, but offers instead better pacing, and slightly more action.

Between the two entrances to Southwest Territory is Demon. It's a meager looping ride, from the 1970s (yes, read that as "primitive"), and is not worth riding unless it has no line at all. Be warned, though, that the majority of the queue is behind the ride, so you may not know how long it will take to board until you're trapped in line. Try instead heading down to the Iron Wolf, a stand-up looping coaster that is located in the back of the park, where Yukon Territory ends and County Fair begins. This ride also has a slow loading process, so be prepared, although it won't be as bad as the two shuttle coasters. Next door, the huge, white American Eagle wooden racer stands tall and proud, and hopefully running both sides (a one-side operation can make the line deadly). The huge queue house for the ride has two lines, so be careful to choose the side you want (at press time, one side offered trains facing backwards).

In theory, you've now beaten the majority of crowds to all the major rides that one comes to this park for (in theory, because all it takes is one of those rides to be closed to throw off the entire plot). Return to the main entrance by the Columbia carousel. You're now going to do the park the way the designers originally planned you to, except you're not going to just go from one ride to the next. There *are* things worth skipping.

Although the carousel is not an antique, it does have the distinction of being the world's tallest carousel. Give it a whirl if you like that sort of thing. You won't have to ride the observation tower nearby, as the park property isn't actually big enough to overwhelm from that high up, and the surrounding town is just that—a sprawling, surrounding town. On a clear day, you might catch a view of Chicago's office towers in the distance, however. Next to the tower is Space Shuttle America, an embarrassing motion simulator that is most definitely not worth even a five minute wait.

Nestled in the trees a bit further down the midway is a must ride for the entire family. Whizzer, a family coaster and one of the park's original rides, is an Anton Schwarzkopf "speedracer" steel coaster. Schwarzkopf is considered the father of the steel looping coaster, and this model, most assuredly without loops, is a fun, twisting

Cave dwelling Demon towers over the old west at Six Flags Great America.
(*Credit: Frank De Santis*)

frolic that is the perfect family ride. (In fact, in 2002, the park announced that it would be removed to install the ride that was eventually announced as Superman. There was such a frenzy to save it, the park instead removed a 170-foot-tall, seven-loop coaster—Shockwave, which was the tallest coaster in the world when it debuted in 1988.

Feel free to bypass the flat spinning rides you'll pass in Hometown Square, as they are not worth standing in line for at all (they're there so that others will, hopefully, and keep the lines down on the big rides). Head back into Southwest Territory and hop on board Giant Drop, a heartpounding few seconds of a ride that just might surprise you in its ability to thrill in such a short ride time.

Check out the lines for Raging Bull and Viper, and if they're not too long, take another spin on those as well.

You'll be back in County Fair in your counterclockwise stroll around the park, home to American Eagle. If you didn't manage to get on both tracks, and have the desire to do so, give it a shot now. Be prepared, though—depending on volume and traffic patterns, there is a time during the day when both counterclockwise- and clockwise-travelling guests all collide, and it's at the American Eagle, so check it all out before you get on the line. If it's a long wait, just keep in mind you already got aboard when there was no one in this section of the park yet.

You've already done Iron Wolf, so keep on walking into Yukon Territory, home to the park's children's areas, as well as a few decent restaurants (barbecued beef, anyone?). This is also the area that contains one of the park's flume entrances, the other being in the Yankee Harbor section (both flumes intertwine, in a fascinating layout). The park's rapids ride is also near the border of Yankee Harbor and the park's final section, Orleans Place, a very French-looking, New Orleans, Louisiana turn-of-the-century themed section that is now home to the Superman ride (Six Flags tries to keep up with logical theming, it really does, but sometimes space just doesn't allow it).

Hopefully, your day at Six Flags Great America won't be too frustrating because of the layout. But here's one tidbit that might get your dander up. At most parks, the main gate area is filled with shops that allow you to visit the park all day without having to worry about having to carry packages. Not here. While there is a last minute outdoor counter, it only has a very limited amount of merchandise, and because of the layout of the park, it's not as if you can now "run" to a shop deep within the park and pick up something you might have taken a fancy to along the way. Your only solutions are to either forgo shopping, hope that the items you want are at the main gate stand (or in a shop in either Orleans Place or Hometown Square, the two sections closest to the main gate), or to make a third go-round in the middle of the day exclusively geared toward shopping and dining. Afterward, you can either rent a locker at the main gate or run out to your car.

Hopefully, a day spent here will be in optimum conditions, and the great ride experiences will more than make up for any disappointments.

SIX FLAGS ST. LOUIS

I-44 and Six Flags Road
Eureka, Missouri 63025
314-938-4800
www.sixflags.com
Admission: $39
Operating Schedule: Mid-April through Halloween, weekends only

Park History

Opening in 1971 as Six Flags Over Mid-America, this was the last park that the Six Flags Theme Park chain actually built from scratch. It was intended to outdo all other parks in its class, and was centered in the middle of the country so that it could become a major tourist destination, easily reached by residents of both coasts. While those plans didn't quite work out the way they were intended, this park, with its expansive midways, lush landscaping, and overall beauty is one of the more pleasant theme parks in the country, with a terrific collection of rides and attractions.

Major Attractions

The Boss—Wooden terrain coaster

Screamin' Eagle—Wooden terrain coaster

Mr. Freeze—Steel linear induction motor launch coaster

Scooby Doo's Scary Swamp—Dark ride

Colossus—Towering ferris wheel

Batman The Ride—Steel inverted, outside-looping coaster

Getting There

Located on I-44, in Allenton, Missouri, just west of St. Louis. Take exit 261/Six Flags Road right into the parking lot. The park is very visible from the interstate.

Planning to Go

As with all other Six Flags parks, a season pass is recommended. Six Flags has major price reduction deals with food chains and local businesses. Call the park for exact details.

Beginning Your Day

This park jumps out at you as you approach it from either direction on I-44. It's situated on a hillside, with both the huge wooden coasters The Boss and Screamin' Eagle at the uppermost sections of the park, towering over everything else in sight. Arrive early, to secure a parking spot close to the main gate, and try to plan your visit for early in the season on a Sunday, or early in the week when the park begins daily operation. Try to avoid busy summer Saturdays completely, as the park can get overwhelming when it's too crowded (that's both for the guests and the staff!).

In the Park

The first two parks in the Six Flags chain (SF Over Texas and SF Over Georgia) had several design issues when they opened (like narrow midways, and not enough capacity), so the intention with this park was to correct them all. The first difference with this park is right at the main entrance. It's wide, expansive, very open, and leads into a large plaza inside the main gate, filled with shops, snack food counters, and places to congregate. Two interlocking flumes were built, as were two interlocking mine train roller coasters (one of which was removed, served as Thunder Express at Dollywood

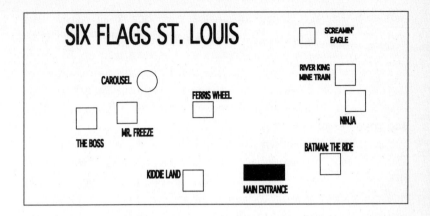

theme park in Tennessee, and now lives as Big Bad John at Magic Springs in Arkansas).

There are a few major attractions near the main gate, which is where everyone will head once inside the park. What you're going to do is head in a different direction.

At the row of shops that comprise the Looney Tunes Shoppe, directly behind the small fountain in the entrance plaza, turn left, then right, and head on up the hill next to the huge building that is the Palace Theatre. The entire park is on a hillside, so most of your walking as you go deeper into the park will be uphill. Keep heading that way, past the Colossus ferris wheel (on your left) and into the British section of the park. Head straight for The Boss (the unpainted, natural wood coaster). This is one of the newer rides in the park, and while it's in the back of the park, it's the one that will attract the most attention. It's a huge terrain ride, beginning with several enormous drops (the first of which is 150 feet tall). Passengers are amazed by this series of drops that all seem to be as big as the last, and are stunned when suddenly, the ride shifts into a swift out-and-back with the train roaring over a series of rabbit hops until it reaches a ferocious helix finale. Enjoy this ride a few times, as it won't have a shorter line at any other time of the day.

Next, head to Illinois, at the highest point in the park (to your left as you leave The Boss). This area is home to the majestic

Screamin' Eagle, a classic out-and-back wooden roller coaster that features a first drop of 89 feet and a third drop of 92 feet (also enabled by the same sort of terrain that The Boss rests upon). Eagle is a frantically paced, relentless ride that is perhaps more suited for families than its newer brother. If you got right up the hill to these two rides, you'll have no problems with lines on either for a while, and you can enjoy multiple rides on each.

Now, head back down the hill on the same path you came up, and at Colossus, make a hard right into DC Comics Plaza. This is the home of Mr. Freeze, a steel shuttle looping coaster that uses linear induction motors to launch the train from 0–70 mph in four seconds. It's a brief, but thrilling experience, with the train careening through an inversion and a tight turn high in the air, and climbing a 90-degree, 225-foot-tall tower, only to plummet backwards through the same course. Although the ride can only operate one train, it has a station that houses two loading docks, with a transfer track, which increases the capacity greatly, since one train is on the course, while the other is loading. It's a fascinating process to witness and it solved the dilemma of how to not have low capacity on single-track forward-and-backward shuttles.

Now, cut across the park, right in front of the Palace Theatre, just to the right of the entrance. Here, the remaining half of the River King Mine Ride resides. It's a fun family mine train-type roller coaster which will develop horrendous lines, since it's the one coaster in the park that everyone (children through grandparents) seems to be interested in riding. With any luck, you've paced yourself well enough so that you can hit it before it grows too long a line. Next to River King, the looping coaster Ninja awaits, but if you're smart, you won't waste your time with this minor attraction that is almost antiquated in the scheme of looping roller coasters. Only ride it if it has no line at all, or bypass it for now and check back later in the evening.

Your one major wait in line will probably be for Batman The Ride, the inverted, outside-looping steel coaster featuring ski-lift-

Climbing Mr. Freeze's "spike" at Six Flags St. Louis. (*Credit: Frank De Santis*)

style seating. This major thriller is located just inside the main gate, and it will be the first thing people ride once in the park, and also the last thing. If you hit it about midday, you'll probably get the shortest wait, but with people tending these days to arrive at parks throughout the day, it won't be that much shorter at any time. And if you think you've ridden this ride at another Six Flags park, guess again. This version is a mirror image, but amazingly enough is quite a different experience.

You've already conquered all the park's major thrill rides, so return to the main gate. You're going to experience this park now the way it was meant to be experienced. This is a very well-rounded park, with offerings for all, and not heavy on any one type of entertainment. This is a park to be savored like a fine wine, best enjoyed leisurely.

Now is the time to head on into Hurricane Harbor water park, included in the price of admission, and entered just to the right of the main entrance area. It's a full service water park, offering quite a nice selection of water-based attractions. It is never recommended that a one-day visit to a theme park should include more than two hours in a water park, as attractions in both parks will be forfeited, but if you just want to cool off quickly, this is a good way to do it.

Otherwise, browse the shops located in the main entrance plaza, and watch fudge and taffy being made right before your eyes at the candy shop. Just to the left of the plaza is First Cone, an ice cream shop featuring hand dipped, delicious ice cream served in warm waffle cones. It honors the fact that the 1904 St. Louis World's Fair was where this treat was invented. Other delicious food items can also be found in this area, or if you're not ready to eat, hop on board the Moon Antique Cars, a great family attraction that fits in with the 1904 theme of the section.

As you continue along the path past the antique cars, to your left is Looney Tunes Land, the section of the park dedicated to children. As kiddie areas go, this one is just so-so, but hopefully, the kids won't notice. It's colorful and enjoyable, with lots of visual stimulation. Further along are a pair of log flumes, both of which offer a fun splash—but not too much of one. You've already done Mr. Freeze, so head for Scooby Doo's Scary Swamp, a dark ride featuring everyone's favorite ghost hunting canine. Follow this up with a soaring trip on the huge Colossus ferris wheel.

Heading up the hill again, into the British section, carousel lovers will rejoice over the park's classic antique merry-go-round, and once this rather passive beauty is enjoyed, the park's rapids offer a more rambunctious experience, as does The Boss, which might just be ready for another go-round.

Now, it's back to Illinois, the location of a few spinning flat rides, as well as a shoot-the-chutes water ride. Try one of the Chicago hot dogs in this area (complete with a pickle spear right on the bun with the dog).

There is a terminal for the park's train station located in Illinois, right in front of the Rush Street Flyer thrill ride. If you love park train rides, by all means hop on board, but don't think that you're going to be saving walk time by taking the train to the next station. Incredibly, although the train virtually circles the entire park, because of the hilly terrain and the location of the park's entrance, both of the stations for the train are located within view of each other. You can actually walk from one to the other in about one minute.

Be sure to take time to stroll through the shops throughout the park, especially the ones in the Missouri section, featuring down home crafts, from wood carving to candle making. The section is one of the more peaceful in any theme park, anywhere.

Six Flags St. Louis allows guests to enter queue lines right up 'til park closing, so plan on being at either The Boss or Screamin' Eagle around that time, for an even more incredible night time experience. This will also allow you to leave the park later and miss the rush, and you won't be caught in the traffic that can reach epic proportions as guests attempt to get back on the interstate.

Spend your last remaining minutes shopping at the stores nearest the main gate. They will have just about all that is for sale in the park, and will further delay your exit, enabling you to avoid the traffic.

SIX FLAGS WORLDS OF ADVENTURE

1060 N. Aurora Road
Aurora, Ohio 44202
330-562-7131
www.sixflags.com
Admission: $40
Operating Schedule: Early May through Halloween

Park History

One of the oldest parks in the country, Six Flags Worlds of Adventure began life in 1888 as the classic amusement park Geauga Lake. This privately owned park became part of the Funtime Park chain in the 1970s, which eventually was purchased by Premier Parks, which then purchased the Six Flags Theme Park chain. The park underwent major expansions once it became a Premier Park, eventually being re-branded Six Flags Ohio. This moniker was not to last, however, and the park finally became Six Flags Worlds of Adventure in 2000 with the purchase and addition of Sea World of Ohio, which shared space on the lake with the amusement park. The total park now covers 750 acres, making it one of the largest regional parks in the country, and offers three different types of experiences: a wild animal park, Hurricane Harbor water park, and the huge ride park.

Major Attractions

The Villain—Wooden roller coaster
Batman Knight Flight—Giant steel, floorless looping coaster
Superman Ultimate Escape—Linear induction, inverted shuttle
X-Flight—Steel flying coaster
Animal Adventures—Sea life and mammal attractions
Hurricane Harbor—Water park

Getting There

Take the Ohio Turnpike to exit 13, then take state road 43 N. Follow signs into Aurora and the park.

Planning to Go

A Six Flags season pass is essential.

The most important thing to remember about this park is that it used to be two separate, full-day parks that combined to make one super park. If you expect to see and do everything there is in the now huge, sprawling park, you must plan for a two-day visit. As with all parks, attempt to make it a weekend early in the season, or early or late during daily operations on a weekday.

Beginning Your Day

Tips for beginning your day at Six Flags Worlds of Adventure begin with your drive to the park. First, you'll more than likely be travelling through the town of Solon. Follow the posted speed limit signs *very* closely. The town is a speed trap, and the speed limits change every few hundred feet.

Also, because of the combination of the two parks, there are now two separate entrances with two separate parking lots. If you're looking to concentrate more on the rides, use the North Gate lot, which is the location of the old Geauga Lake entrance. If you want to concentrate more on animals, use the South Gate lot (the old entrance to Sea World). Both gates will bring you into the park, and you can then travel between both sections either on foot, or by ferry boat across the lake.

In the Park

Since this book focuses mainly on the ride sections of parks, we're going to enter Six Flags Worlds of Adventure through the North Gate, where the ride section of the park is located.

SIX FLAGS WORLDS OF ADVENTURE

RAGING WOLF BOBS

VILLAIN

BATMAN KNIGHT FLIGHT

ANIMAL PARK

DOUBLE LOOP

SERIAL THRILLER

FERRY TO ANIMAL PARK

FERRY TO RIDE PARK

BIG DIPPER   HURRICANE HARBOR   LOONEY TUNES BOOMTOWN

MAIN GATE

X-FLIGHT   SUPERMAN ULTIMATE ESCAPE

Once through the gate, turn right and make your way directly to Superman Ultimate Escape. This is a shuttle inverted coaster, and has one train, so it also has low capacity. You'll need to ride it first thing and get it out of the way before the crowds arrive. You might not get the chance to ride it again all day, so take a few rides if you are able to do so without waiting in line too long.

Then immediately board X-Flight. This is a flying coaster, featuring vehicles that hang the passengers in a flying position both above and below the track. The loading process can take a while, since passengers get a bit nervous about how to fit into the restraints properly, so you'll also want to get on this one quickly.

Once you've accomplished this, you'll need to head right to the Big Dipper wooden roller coaster. This classic wooden ride, dating from 1926, was once the world's longest roller coaster, and now provides a rambunctious journey through what used to be the entire park many, many years ago. Unfortunately, it frequently runs only one train, so savor your rides, and get as many as you can.

Now, move back in the direction of the main gate, and head to the Coyote Creek section. To the right of the midway is Serial Thriller, a suspended looping coaster, which can be fun if it's running two trains (otherwise, the wait will dull your brain and you won't enjoy the ride). To the left of the midway, in Coyote Creek, is a great water flume, plus a wooden coaster known as Villain. It's a

Coaster after coaster line the shore of Geauga Lake at Six Flags Worlds of Adventure. (*Credit: Frank De Santis*)

high-speed, wreckless experience, careening over rabbit hops and relentless twists. An unusual feature is that although it's a wooden coaster, its structure is lattice work steel, which saves on building space and actually creates a more trouble-free, easier-to-maintain ride. Right next to Villain is the aptly but unimaginatively named Double Loop. This is a primitive design, built in the 1970s, and won't thrill anyone but the easiest to please.

Next up is Gotham City, and the awesome Batman Knight Flight. This is a floorless coaster, meaning that the passenger vehicles have been stripped right down to a simple seat on wheels. Legs dangle directly over the track, but while the vehicles are very different and open, the ride itself is a good old looping coaster, the kind that have been around for years (although not quite in such a dynamic way). Knight Flight is considered by many to be one of the better floorless coaster experiences, with intense tight turns, high speeds, and a bold layout.

The white wooden coaster in what used to be the rear area of the park is called Raging Wolf Bobs, and is inspired by a classic wooden coaster that existed at Chicago's famed Riverview Park. It's definitely tamer than the original, and in fact is probably the mildest ride in the entire park.

Now, you've reached what used to be the end of the park, and in former years, you had no choice but to turn around and head back the way you came. Now, however, you can continue around Raging Wolf Bobs, and follow the path into Happy Harbor, the entrance portal between the theme park and the animal park.

At this point, you have two choices. You can continue into the animal park for a one-day, incomplete visit, or you can head back through the theme park and do all the attractions you missed (which are many), and save the animal section for a second day's visit (don't forget, you also have a water park to visit). For clarity's sake, we'll continue into the animal section, and make one full round of the entire park, but you really should want to make this a two-day park stint. In nearly every other theme park with this much going on, the parks are usually separate, gated attractions with combo tickets available, and guests can visit each on separate days. Here at Six Flags Worlds of Adventure, with all three parks included in the one admission, you're almost encouraged to see it all in one day, and that's impossible. You'll be shortchanging yourself and the park, and probably won't get enough out of any of the sections to satisfy yourself.

Animal Adventures includes a wide variety of attractions. Must see exhibits include Shouka, a killer whale, and Tiger Island, a natural habitat where visitors can witness big cats doing their thing. Various other animal exhibits, shows, and attractions abound in the wildlife side of the park. Most are offered as scheduled entertainment, so it would be wise to check the times for the exhibits you want to see, and make sure you get to the exhibit early. Because of the nature of scheduled attractions, it's best to plan your journey through the wildlife side according to the show and exhibit times, as you won't be able to do them at your whim, and you won't be able to rush through them, either.

Continuing the journey around the lake will eventually lead you to the ferry landing, and the return trip to the ride side of the park. Conveniently, the ride side ferry dock is located between the park's Looney Tunes Boomtown children's section and Hurricane Harbor water park. If you've been hauling children around, they're probably exhausted by now and won't have any interest in the kiddie rides, and you'll probably be too exhausted to enjoy the water park (swimming, climbing stairs, and wading in wave pools requires energy, you know), so you may just want to do a few of the attractions near the Big Dipper roller coaster and head on out, back to your hotel, to rest up.

If you do manage a two-day visit to Six Flags Worlds of Adventure, follow the theme park plan as outlined previously, but at Raging Wolf Bobs, head back through the theme park and do what you missed. Spend the afternoon in the water park, and do the main attractions in the theme park again at your leisure in the evening hours. On the second day, park in the south lot, enter Animal Adventures directly, and spend a leisurely day visiting all the animal attractions. If you wish to experience a ride or two, hop on the ferry, and try to keep your riding to the front of the park, near the main gate areas. There are many wonders to behold at this superpark, and they can't be rushed.

WORLDS OF FUN

4545 Worlds of Fun Avenue
Kansas City, Missouri 64161
816-454-4545
www.worldsoffun.com
Admission: $35
Operating Schedule: Late April through October

Park History

Built by Lamar Hunt, owner of the Kansas City Royals baseball team, this park opened in 1973. This smaller, friendlier theme park was eventually purchased by Cedar Fair, LP, owners of Cedar Point, who began its transformation through a series of expansions into a *larger* smaller, friendlier theme park.

Major Attractions

Mamba—200-foot-tall non-looping steel coaster

Timber Wolf—Wooden roller coaster

Detonator—Rocket launching air compression thrill ride tower

Getting There

Take I-435 to exit 54, the east loop. The park is right next to the interstate.

Planning to Go

Worlds of Fun is adjacent to Oceans of Fun, a huge water park. A separate admission is required for both, but there is a combination ticket available. While this chapter will only focus on the theme park, if you do plan on visiting both, allot two days, as you can't see all the parks have to offer in only one. Coupons and money saving tips are available at the park's Web site.

Beginning Your Day

This park has a huge parking lot to allow entrance into both theme park and water park. Make sure you park in the section of the lot closest to the appropriate entrance. You might notice that the main entrance is a bit nondescript. This is due to the fact that the current main entrance used to be the park's back gate; the original main entrance is no longer in use. In order to experience the park the way it was intended, enter the park, head down to the main midway, and turn right, walking past the Orient Express roller coaster, to

The thrill ride Thunder Hawk at Worlds of Fun. (*Credit: Courtesy of Worlds of Fun and Oceans of Fun*)

the Americana section. The entrance plaza, complete with the usual fountain, shops, and restaurants are all still there, just past Sky Coaster, while the actual entrance is now home to a go-kart track. Starting off from here will enable you to experience the park as it was originally intended, a tour through the lands featured in the Jules Verne classic, *Around the World in 80 Days*.

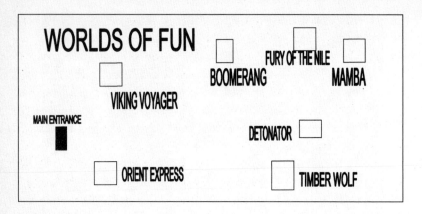

In the Park

Now that you're at the original entrance, you've got a head start on things.

If you've been reading each section of this book carefully, you'll have noticed that it is never recommended that a guest head right to the major ride nearest the main gate. Once upon a time at this park, that ride would have been Timber Wolf, the park's famed wooden roller coaster. The new entrance entices everyone to head to Orient Express, which you've just passed up, so now you're free to board Timber Wolf with gleeful abandon.

Timber Wolf is a twisting, diabolical airtime machine, with a mid-course helix and wild direction changes. It appeared in many top ten lists when it made its 1990 debut. You'll want to ride it a few times, then head on over to Detonator, also in the Americana section of the park. It's an air-compression launching tower ride, with vehicles that dangle passengers' legs in the air. After that, it's on to Africa to conquer the monstrous Mamba.

Mamba, a 200-foot-tall non-looping hyper coaster, uses terrain to its advantage, so that the second drop is almost as long as the first. The far end of the ride offers a super-intense helix, and a wild series of rabbit hops comprise the finale.

You might opt to get wet at this time, so hop on the nearby Fury of the Nile, a heavily themed rapids ride. Passing under the park's train tracks, you'll find yourself in Europa and next to yet another Boomerang shuttle coaster, which, if it has any line at all, you should take a pass on. By the way, this is another park designed in a circular layout, but the Europa section is smack dab in the middle, acting almost as a hub, and allowing access to other sections. Be careful to stay generally to your right in this section, or else you'll wind up back in Americana, having missed two entire sections of the park that are only accessible from the outer midway.

After you go under another section of railroad track, you're in Scandinavia, home to a large collection of flat, spinning rides, as well as a great flume ride, Viking Voyager. Next up is the Orient, home to the Orient Express, the huge black and red looping coaster you bypassed on your way into the park. This was quite a ride in its day (it's over twenty years old) and was the first coaster to feature a "kamikaze curve" (double-looping pretzel knot).

You've probably beaten the crowds around the park, and it's also probably still early in the day. So enjoy the rest of the park at your leisure, taking in some shows, enjoying the variety of flat rides, and browsing through the plethora of shops. Each section has not only park souvenir items, but also gift items pertaining to the region the section is themed after.

Food items throughout the park also feature selections that pertain to the themed area that houses the restaurant.

Obviously, this is a park that is a bit easier to do, offers a less frantic pace, and can be enjoyed at a more leisurely pace than the giant parks. Enjoy it for its many sweet, simple pleasures.

6

THE SOUTH

BUSCH GARDENS TAMPA BAY
BUSCH GARDENS WILLIAMSBURG
PARAMOUNT'S KINGS DOMINION
SIX FLAGS OVER GEORGIA
SIX FLAGS OVER TEXAS
UNIVERSAL STUDIOS ORLANDO

BUSCH GARDENS TAMPA BAY

3605 Bougainvillea
Tampa, Florida 33612
813-987-5000
www.buschgardens.com
Admission: $50
Operating Schedule: Park open daily, year round. Hours vary depending
  on season—most days, park opens at either 9 A.M. or 10 A.M. Call for
  exact operating days and hours.

Park History

This park started its life as a zoo/animal exhibit park, with a few
other rides and attractions, in 1959, all of it surrounding an
Anheuser-Busch brewery. It began expanding with the addition of

new rides and attractions, including several spectacular thrill rides, and eventually squeezed out the brewery in favor of even more attractions. It is now one of the best entertainment centers in the country, with more to offer the older teen, adult, and senior crowds than any of the parks in nearby Orlando combined.

Major Attractions

Kumba—Huge steel looping coaster

Montu—Huge inverted steel looping coaster

Gwazi—Dual-track, dueling wooden roller coaster

Edge of Africa—An African safari

Rhino Rally—Off-road vehicle animal encounter, with wet and wild water thrill ride

Tanganyika Tidal Wave—River boat journey with a perilous splashdown finale.

Getting There

Take I-275 to exit 33, Busch Boulevard exit, or I-75 to exit 265, Fowler Avenue. Follow signs to the park.

Planning to Go

The park is open year round, and is certainly less crowded during the winter months, but certain rides close for annual maintenance during this time, so call and check to see which ones will be down at the time of your planned visit. The park also has limited hours of operation during the winter, with closing times around 5 or 6 P.M. Hours are extended in summer.

This park has one of the highest gate admissions of any park in the country, and it's not easy to get a discount. On occasion, there will be a fast food promotion of some sort, but it won't be for any substantial savings. It's clear that the park wants to get every dime it can from you in admission! (This is, after all, central Florida, home to the world's biggest tourist destination.)

One method of savings is to buy tickets online at the park's Web site. You'll be able to get up to 20% off the price, depending on how far in advance you make your purchase (and yes, that still leaves you with a $40 admission price tag).

Very few people visit central Florida for a short time—most are there to visit all the attractions that comprise Theme Park Central. A good deal, if you do plan to visit everything, is the 5 Park Orlando Flex Ticket, good for admission to not only Busch Gardens Tampa, but also Sea World Orlando, Universal Studios Florida, Universal's Islands of Adventure, and Wet N' Wild Orlando. It's $202.95 for all five parks, a savings of about $40.

Unlike every other major theme park chain, a season pass purchased at the park doesn't automatically include unlimited visits to other parks in the chain—you have to pay additional upcharges for that (the silver pass, the gold pass, the platinum pass). All passes at least offer free parking and certain minor discounts in the park, including on food and merchandise.

Because of the high ticket price, which does not go down at times when the park is open fewer hours, you'll probably want to plan your visit for when the park has full operating hours, even if it is a bit more crowded. A bigger crowd does not necessarily mean longer lines, as the big thrill rides can be ridden without much of a problem while much of the crowd is visiting the animals, one of the major attractions in the park.

Beginning Your Day

You *must* arrive at this park well before the posted opening time. There is only one small lot on near the main gate, and you *want* to be parked in it, by all means. Arriving later means you'll be directed to lots across the street, which are not only a long walk away, but must be accessed by tram. You don't want to be a slave to the tram service, even though it runs frequently. If you choose to go back to

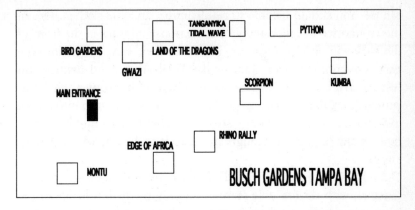

the car at all, you won't want to have to spend an hour to do so. This early in the day, the main gate will not have a major delay with long lines, either, and you should breeze right in.

Please note: *None* of the major rides allow any loose items to be carried on board, and they won't let you leave them behind in the station. Each major ride has a set of lockers set up right outside the entrance, designed to store these items during your ride. The cost for this can add up during the day, so do not under any circumstances carry anything into the park with you that you can't fit securely in a pocket or fanny pack. This includes purses, by the way, so ladies, you'll need to downsize.

In the Park

The first section you'll be in after you enter the park is Morocco, a land of shops, street bazaars, and restaurants. If you've arrived early, you'll want to grab a cup of coffee and a pastry here before you begin your travels. Once you're ready to begin your safari through Africa, head through the Myombe Reserve, Nairobi, and Timbuktu, all the way to the Congo, home of Kumba, the large blue looping coaster in the back of the park.

This ride is a seven-inversion, sit-down looper, designed so exquisitely that it is smooth as glass, and one of the ultimate thrill rides. It offers intense pacing, and a finale with an underground tunnel. You should be able to ride Kumba, and most other rides in the Congo section repeatedly, as attractions and rides in the front of the park will occupy guests as they make their way further into the park. One not to miss is Tanganyika Tidal Wave, a boat ride on an African river, complete with scenery and animatronics that ends with a shoot-the-chutes plunge down a hair-raising drop into a pool of water that is guaranteed to soak everyone! During midday hours, hop on the Skyride in Congo and take it to Egypt, where Montu awaits.

Montu is one of the world's largest inverted, outside-looping coasters, with ski-lift-style seating. Heavily themed, it is one of the more intense coasters there is, with another seven inversions, underground tunnels, a few near-misses with concrete walls, and even more below-grade dives. Montu is located close enough to the front gate that it's possible, by the time you've arrived to take a few spins, that mostly everyone will be on their way to the back of the park to ride Kumba.

Near the Skyride Terminal is Edge of Africa. This is an up close and personal safari through the Serengeti Plains, where you'll be able to experience African wildlife at close range. You'll now have two choices. Either head back to Nairobi for Rhino Rally, or back to Morocco, where just past the main entrance is the park's third major roller coaster, Gwazi. Let's opt for Gwazi, since it's also adjacent to a children's area.

Gwazi is a dual-track wooden coaster, with completely different layouts on each side. Gwazi Lion and Gwazi Tiger, as the tracks are respectively named, essentially share only a loading dock. Each takes off on a different path as soon as they are dispatched, and there are several moments when trains from the opposing sides come within inches of each other, appearing as if they will have a head-on collision. It's a beautifully designed and engineered ride. *Be warned*, however, that the loading procedures on this ride, implemented by the park, are perhaps the slowest and most frustrating on any coaster, anywhere. There is so seldom a train running along the

Zooming through the palm trees at Florida's Busch Gardens. (*Credit: Frank De Santis*)

course that park guests frequently think the ride is closed. Even a short line for the ride can take up a half-hour of your day. You'll want to ride this a lot, but you'll waste so much time doing it, it's not worth it.

Across from Gwazi are the Bird Gardens. This tranquil section of the park features beautiful floral displays and exotic birds from around the world. It's a great place to relax, if you feel it's time to do so. Next door, Land of the Dragons is a children's play area with rides, colorfully themed to an enchanted land of dragons, fair maidens, and a world that exists only in our imagination. (A note on kiddie rides: Busch Gardens doesn't have the usual kiddie ride section. As a *very* nice touch, kiddie rides are situated throughout the park, interspersed with adult rides, so that each area contains rides for all ages.)

Continuing along, one arrives back in Stanleyville, home to Stanley Falls, a great family water flume; Python, a small double corkscrew coaster; numerous animal displays, and shops. Next, the Congo section contains more rides, the Kumba roller coaster, and a train stop to take you on a journey around the park. Timbuktu is next, and this area is home to the most flat rides in the park, all of varying intensity, a few kiddie rides, and the Scorpion roller coaster, a single looping affair that manages to be very good, despite its small size. The section also contains a dolphin show, which is very entertaining as well as educational, and the Festhaus, a cavernous building with a Germanic theme, where guests can get not only a high-quality meal (from giant sandwiches to pasta to pizza), but they can also enjoy one of the park's signature shows, a German festival dance that invites guests to participate. This is an enjoyable way to spend a few moments resting, eating, and smiling.

Leaving Timbuktu, you'll arrive in Nairobi again, and it's time to experience Rhino Rally. This is an incredible attraction, featuring a journey in off-road vehicles, that take visitors on a safari where they get very close to live animals. It all ends when the vehicle crosses a pontoon bridge, that is suddenly swept away in a water surge, which then turns the attraction into a super-charged thrill ride.

As you make your way around the park, you'll notice that each section relies highly on its animal displays and exhibits. Busch Gardens is one of the highest-rated zoos in the country. The animals aren't just here for eye-candy or theming; they're here because they're the main focus of the park. The rides are actually the secondary focus, although the park has some of the best.

Unfortunately, because the animals *are* the main focus of the park, operating hours here are more comparable to those of a zoo rather than a theme park. Closing time can be as early as 5 P.M., and hours aren't necessarily extended that late even during the summer season. This is a park where you'll want to spend lots of time (you can always plan a second day). You'll rarely get to be in the park after dark, so be prepared to have an evening to spend with still-wired members of your group searching for something more to do.

BUSCH GARDENS WILLIAMSBURG

1 Busch Gardens Boulevard
Williamsburg, Virginia 23185
804-253-3350
www.buschgardens.com
Admission: $43
Operating Schedule: Late March through late October. Park opens
    10 A.M., with closing times as late as 10 P.M. during summer months.

Park History

The park opened in 1975 as the latest addition to the Anheuser-
Busch's family of theme parks, designed to attract tourists to the
company's breweries. The park is perhaps the best-themed theme
park in the country—you'll actually feel as if you've travelled back to
Old World Europe while strolling the streets and villages (it's hard
to call them midways and themed areas) located here. Seven different countries are represented, along with a section that is decidely
historical North America.

Major Attractions

Alpengeist—World's tallest steel inverted roller coaster
Big Bad Wolf—Suspended roller coaster
Loch Ness Monster—Double interlocking loop steel roller
    coaster
Escape From Pompeii—Heavily themed indoor/outdoor shoot-
    the-chutes water ride with special effects.
Apollo's Chariot—Non-looping steel hyper coaster

Getting There

Take I-64 to exit 243A, and follow state road 199 to Rt. 60 to the
park's entrance, on your right.

Planning to Go

You'll find occasional discounts at fast food chains or supermarket chains. You can also purchase tickets online, in advance, at the park's Web site, which offers a slight discount.

Busch Gardens Williamsburg is one of the rare theme parks that actually offers a rain check to come back the next day in cases of wet weather (although, unless it's an electrical storm, wet weather is probably the best time to experience the park to the fullest). The park is not crowded very early in the season, nor on Friday evenings during September and October.

The majority of tourists at the park are also in town for a few days to experience the attractions of Colonial Williamsburg, so the park gets packed during the summer months. Weekdays are always best, but don't expect a huge drop off in attendance, as that's the usual time for vacationing families to be here as well. Sundays are the least crowded of the two weekend days, by far.

Beginning Your Day

Busch Gardens Williamsburg has a hellish parking lot arrangement. Rather than one big lot, the park has several smallish lots, situated around the property, with only two next to the main gate (and therefore within walking distance). The first lot is reserved for bus parking and VIP parking (don't let the name fool you—it's an excuse to charge extra money for parking close). Arrive at least one hour before the park is scheduled to open—you might just be directed into the VIP lot, but failing that, you'll be parked in France, which is the next parking depot in line, and also provides access to the main gate. All the other lots are a tram ride away, and you are not permitted to walk to these lots, even if you wanted to! The ticket booths are located a bit of a walk from the main entrance, but it's a lovely area to sit and enjoy, relax, or plan your day.

FYI: this park opens its themed sections at various times throughout the day. Just because the park opens at 10 A.M., that doesn't mean the entire park will necessarily be available.

BUSCH GARDENS WILLIAMSBURG

BIG BAD WOLF

WILD MAUS

ALPENGEIST

LE SCOOT
FLUME

LAND OF THE DRAGONS

RHINE RIVER CRUISE

LE MANS
RACEWAY

ROMAN RAPIDS

ESCAPE FROM POMPEII

LOCH NESS MONSTER

CLYDESDALE STABLES

APOLLO'S CHARIOT

MAIN ENTRANCE

In the Park

The first area inside the main gate is Banbury Cross, the section themed to Olde England. There are dozens of shops here, as well as a restaurant that serves breakfast and pastry items. Grab a snack if you haven't eaten outside the park, and stroll right through to Heatherdowns. Your first close encounter with a roller coaster is waiting.

Right at the top of the hill as you enter Heatherdowns towers a huge yellow tracked steel beast. This is Loch Ness Monster, perhaps one of the most famous roller coasters in the world. It's a double looping ride, with a 115-foot first drop, and a wild indoor helix. If the ride operates all three trains, be prepared to see a train in each interlocking loop simultaneously (this is more for a visual effect on the ground; you hardly know it's happening on the ride itself). This is a great ride, and despite its size, is suitable for many family members. Ride it until a line develops. The park usually allows re-rides if no one is waiting in line.

After leaving Loch Ness, head right and down the huge flight of stairs to the Rhine River area. There is a small pontoon bridge that crosses this beautiful (but man-made) river, and it provides a short-cut across the center of the park to the German area, located in the back half of the park. Be very aware that your steep climb down the

The out of control ski lift, or the saw mill—just two of the insane Busch Gardens attractions. (*Credit: Frank De Santis*)

steps on one side will be met by a shorter flight of stairs on the other side, capped by a steep sloping climb on a path; this might prove difficult for some. You'll only have to do this maneuver once, so grit your teeth and get on with it.

Once at the top of the hill, you'll be in the enchanting Land of the Dragons, a children's play/ride area that is the portal to Rhinefeld, the German-themed section. This section has a host of spinning rides, and three roller coasters designed to test your endurance. The first one you should try is the low-capacity Wild Maus, a small steel coaster with zig-zagging track that tiny four-passenger vehicles zip along at a much faster pace than most would think. Many assume this ride is going to be a piece of cake. The screams from that corner of Rhinefeld belie that notion.

You won't be able to miss the towering steel inverted coaster right near Wild Maus. This is Alpengeist, the world's tallest inverted coaster. Themed around a haunted ski lift, the ride takes passengers 195 feet in the air before dropping them, with legs dangling ski-lift-style, through loops, twists, and turns, some of which are positioned on a hillside and provide even deeper drops than expected. The ride ends with a spiral through a snowy trough that seems to be a lot closer to passengers' shoes than comfort would allow.

Leaving Alpengeist behind, stroll back through Rhinefeld, past the huge Festhaus building, turn left, and head for the station of Big Bad Wolf. This is a fun suspended coaster, with trains hanging below the track, much like Alpengeist (although the trains here don't go through loops—they do, however, swing freely with each turn). The ride starts off with a fun and furious journey through a Bavarian Village, right past the doorways and windows of the tiny hamlet's homes, and ends with a 100-foot climb up a second lift hill, where the train careens down an eighty-foot, steep drop to a terrifying and wet conclusion.

When you exit Big Bad Wolf, head to the right and across the bridge that leads to the two Italian sections, San Marco and Festa Italia. These are the areas that contain most of the park's flat ride selection, and they also include several major ones as well. San Marco is a gorgeous area, with narrow streets, beautiful shops, and a stupendous restaurant that includes a stage show (you won't believe the talent that's on that stage, either). If it's lunch time, here's where you'll want to eat, so check the show schedule to ensure that you'll also be entertained while you dine. Stroll the shop-lined streets after lunch to digest your food, because rides are ahead.

You'll probably want to start off slow, so pass through the San Marco ride selections and head left when you get to the footbridge to Festa Italia. On your left, you'll see a huge building, with an equally huge water trough pouring down from the top. This is Escape From Pompeii, one of the most heavily themed and elaborate water rides you'll ever encounter. Busch Gardens took the simple up, around, and down layout of the standard shoot-the-chute and enclosed and elongated it, so your twenty passenger boat now climbs up the hill and enters the ruined, Italian-flavored building, and is quickly drawn into the eruption of Mount Vesuvius. There's rumbling and shaking, and suddenly columns and statues are falling, and bursting into flames (be prepared, the fire is *hot*), which even travel through the water! After the eruption, your boatload cruises slowly into a misty, dark and quiet area, and suddenly, the wall in front of the boat opens up, and you plunge down a 60-foot drop to a huge splashdown below.

After your hot and wet adventure, head back into San Marco, and this time, cross the footbridge into Festa Italia. More spinning rides wait for you here, as does Apollo's Chariot, a 210-foot-tall non-looping steel coaster. This ride has steep drops and a few nice turns as well, all in open, pedestal-style seating that leaves feet dangling above the floor of the car. It might look intimidating, but it's actually quite suitable for the entire family. No moment of this ride is designed to terrify. Also in the Festa Italia section is Roman Rapids, a river raft ride through Roman ruins that is quite fun, nicely themed, and not in the least bit dry.

There's a stop for the park's train in Festa Italia, so hop on board (because of the park's terrain, the park's train and skyride not only serve as rides, but also very definitely as a means of transportation around the park). Take the train to the next stop, which is located in New France. In New France, you'll have the opportunity to ride the park's flume, known as Le Scoot. Themed as a French Canadian log mill, this is a fun ride, with a buzzsaw included in the finale. And if you're feeling hunger pangs again, the section contains some of the best barbecue you'll ever have in an amusement park.

It's just a short walk into the Aquitaine, an old French themed village. There are plenty of shops here, plus the Le Mans Raceway, a four-track mini race car ride that is loads of fun for the entire family.

Adjacent to the Aquitaine is Jack Hanna's Wild Reserve, a section devoted to the preservation of endangered animals, including the exotic gray wolf. Nearby is Eagle Canyon, a sanctuary for several

American Bald Eagles, all living peacefully in a natural habitat. Finally, there's Ireland, the park's newest themed village. The section is home to even more shops, an authentic Irish pub, and a 3-D motion simulator adventure.

As you make your way back to Heatherdowns and your starting off point, you'll pass through an area housing the Clydesdale Stables. These are the world-famous Anheuser-Busch signature horses, and they're available to visit (although the park doesn't offer horse rides!).

When the sun goes down at Busch Gardens, the lights come up, and the park transforms into an even more beautiful place. Each building in the park has its own outside lighting, as do all the rides, and it tends to be more of an artful, tasteful effect rather than the more garish beauty of most theme parks. All of the park's roller coasters take on a new thrill at night, with sections that are totally in the dark, and if you choose to sit and partake of a snack at one of the outdoor cafés located in each of the villages, you will really feel as if you've been transported back in time to whichever country you happen to be in at the time.

Finish out your visit in Rhinefeld. You won't want to miss the shorter lines on Big Bad Wolf and Alpengeist, and you'll be able to grab a late snack in Festhaus (try to be there for the final show of the day—you'll be sorry if you miss it). Additionally, there are both adult and kiddie flat rides here for every taste, and a huge gift shop to stroll through. You'll be able to make it back to Heatherdowns by boarding the sky ride station located in Rhinefeld, which will take you right back to the front of the park. Be sure to be on the line before park closing time, or else you'll have to walk—if that happens, take the hill and steps leading to the Rhine River only if you feel up to it. Otherwise, head across the bridge to San Marco and gain access to Banbury Cross that way.

The shops and restaurants of Banbury Cross are open late, so feel free to shop and get a snack for the ride home. The outer entry way leading to the parking lots is so peaceful at night that you'll have no idea you just left one of America's top theme parks.

PARAMOUNT'S KINGS DOMINION

16000 Theme Park Way
Doswell, Virginia 23047
804-876-5000
www.kingsdominion.com
Admission: $42
Operating Schedule: Late March through October. Park opens
   at 10:30 A.M., with closing times as late as 10 P.M., depending
   on season.

Park History

The park opened in 1975, a full-fledged theme park expansion of
what was once known as Lion Country Safari. It was a sister park to
Cincinatti's Kings Island, which opened in 1972. Both parks were
owned by Taft Broadcasting, and were later sold to Kings Entertainment. The animal section stayed as a major part of the park,
while the theme park section continued to expand with each season.
Paramount Pictures eventually bought the Kings Entertainment
chain of parks, and expanded them even more—especially this one,
which gained a huge water park, doubled the amount of roller
coasters, and became home to one of the best children's sections in
the theme park world (only rivaled by Paramount's Kings Island).
The park is now home to more wooden roller coasters than any
other park in the world (a total of four), and more launching steel
coasters than any other park as well (three).

The park became a movie star in the 1977 feature *Rollercoaster*, as
actor George Segal played cat and mouse with Timothy Bottoms
throughout the park, with a briefcase filled with blackmail loot.

Major Attractions

   Grizzly—Twisting wooden roller coaster
   Drop Zone—305-foot-tall freefall

Volcano The Blast Coaster—The world's fastest, linear induction motor suspended coaster

Flight of Fear—Totally enclosed linear induction motor launching looping coaster

Hypersonic SLC—Steel air-pressure launching coaster

Hurler—Wooden twisting roller coaster

Rebel Yell—Racing wooden coaster with one side featuring a backwards facing train

Nickelodeon Splat City—Adventure area themed to the popular television network's wet and wild fun

Eiffel Tower—330-foot-tall observation tower that's a one-third scale replica of the original in Paris.

Getting There

Take I-95 to exit 98.

Planning to Go

If you purchase your tickets online at least two days before your visit, you'll get a $3 discount. You'll also find coupons with fast food chains (though infrequently). A season pass, priced at $80, is good for all five North American Paramount Parks, so if you plan to visit another one during your travels, this is a good deal, as it pays for itself in less than two visits.

The park is not all that crowded very early in spring, nor is it very crowded the last full week of August, before Labor Day. Sundays are better than Saturdays, and weekdays early in the season are better than in summer.

The park very rarely runs at less than full capacity, no matter what time of the season, so even on slow days, you'll find it in full swing. The water park, located in the middle of the park and included in admission, eats up crowds during daylight hours.

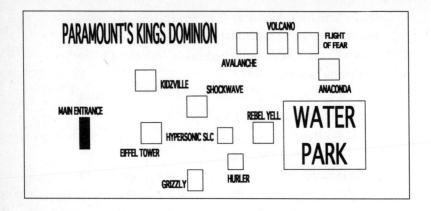

Beginning Your Day

Arrive at the parking lot well before 10 A.M., in order to find a close parking space. You can gain access into the park when you arrive, and you'll be able to stroll through the shops or grab coffee and a pastry for breakfast. Although this is a major theme park, it feels like you should just relax and savor the moment as you would in a much smaller, family-owned park. Like all the Paramount Parks, this one is known for its customer service and friendly employees.

In the Park

The entrance into the park is very similar to the entrance to Paramount's Kings Island, although on a slightly less grandiose scale. Just like Kings Island, you pass through a roofed entrance plaza into International Street, with its amazing fountain and Eiffel Tower backdrop, which makes this the world's second-best theme park entrance dazzler.

The park has an opening time of 10:30 A.M. each day, which is half an hour later than most other theme parks. International Street, however, opens earlier, so you'll be able to do some planning, grab breakfast, and just sit by the fountain enjoying some tranquility before you begin your mad dash around the park.

Plan on being at the far end of International Street, past the Eiffel Tower, before the rope drops and the rest of the park opens. Simply stroll along the fountain, around the Tower, and meet up with the ride-hungry crowds all waiting to be unleashed on the rest of the park. At 10:30 A.M., when the rope drops, head on down the sloping, straight lane and, when you reach the end, turn slightly right. Your first objective of the morning is Hypersonic SLC. This is an air-launching coaster with low capacity, and you want to be one of the first to ride (it's been known to have four-hour lines). You'll be shot from 0–70 m.p.h. in two seconds, and up a completely vertical tower; at the top, there's a 180 degree vertical hairpin, leading to a straight down drop, and into a series of turns and hops. The ride is short but breathtaking.

Nearby, you may also want to get an early ride on Drop Zone, the park's newest attraction. This 305-foot-tall tower carries forty passengers to the top while slowly revolving. Then, all motion stops for a heartpounding moment, and the entire vehicle plummets to earth. It's the tallest ride of its kind in America.

Leaving both of your first high-tech experiences behind, walk directly past the stand-up coaster Shock Wave, and continue on to the Congo section of the park, walking towards the man-made mountain directly ahead. This is Volcano The Blast Coaster, another launching ride that can have an agonizingly long line. The ride features legs dangling, inverted seating, and once you're on board, will slowly leave the station, make a left turn, and rocket into the fastest ground-hugging banked turn you'll ever experience. And that's just for starters. The train hits a second set of linear induction motors and launches straight into the mountain, and, coming out of the top at 155 feet above the earth, executes a corkscrew, then a series of barrel rolls. The ride ends with an eighty-foot plunge back to the ground. This is a short ride that seems to end just when it's getting started, so you won't want to wait too long for it.

Right next door is Flight of Fear, another linear induction launch coaster, but this one is in total darkness. The ride features a space invader theme, and has the tightest layout of any major steel coaster

Lava or roller coaster riders? Volcano The Blast Coaster, Paramount's Kings Dominion. (*Credit: Frank De Santis*)

currently operating. The diabolical course will flip you over three times right at the beginning, after which you'll be sent through a series of twists and dives that will totally disorient you. There's a final inversion right at the end that always takes riders by surprise, especially since you can't see it coming.

If you've successfully boarded each of these attractions, you've already gotten on all the rides that might prove to be troublesome with long lines, so you're now ready to go for the higher capacity rides. Feel free to start with Anaconda, the large looping steel coaster near Flight of Fear. This is a bumpy one, but also includes a dive under the park's lake (the only coaster to actually dive under water in the world). You also might want to check out the Avalanche, a bobsled-style coaster on the other side of Volcano's mountain—it's a family ride, suitable for everyone, and it's loads of fun. The train rides freely in a steel trough, just like a real bobsled.

Walk back the way you came into the area. The stand up Shock

Wave coaster is to your right. You'll need to check the line for this one, as it is also one of the slower moving lines in the park. If it extends anywhere near the ride entrance, forget it 'til later, as it will eat up about an hour of your day. (The restraints on this version of the stand-up coaster are complicated; passengers have a hard time figuring them out, and each "seat" must be adjusted manually for height by a ride attendant). You might have to wait for this one 'til the end of the night if the line has already grown.

You're now headed to the park's three adult wooden roller coasters. First up, past Hypersonic SXLC, is Hurler, a coaster originally themed to the Wayne's World duo of movies (as was an entire section of the park, which nowadays seems to have been rethought). Hurler features an eighty-five-foot drop into a flat-ground-hugging turn, and from there, it has amazing airtime, more fast turns, and a relentless pace that brings you back to the station breathless. In this area, you can also experience Richochet, a wild mouse-style ride with a fifty-foot drop (very uncommon for this type of ride).

When leaving the Hurler/Hypersonic area, to your right is the entrance for Rebel Yell, the park's classic wooden racer. The path to your right is for the forward side, the path to your left is for the backward side. Whichever side you choose, be prepared for a fast and furious ride over a dozen hops and hills, with a great, ninety-foot, very steep first drop. This is a great, thrilling ride that isn't quite tame enough for all members of the family, but is certainly not too much for most to take.

As you leave Rebel Yell, walk toward the Eiffel Tower, staying a bit to your left, and head under the beautiful arbor tunnel. Just past the towering arch of the sky coaster, to the left, is the entrance for Grizzly, the third adult coaster in the park, and the one that has been known to make coaster top ten lists. This is a sinister ride, to say the least, because it begins with a rather tame eighty-five-foot drop, and is followed by a huge, slow flat turn. Then suddenly . . . all heck breaks loose! This is a ride that uses psychology to create thrills, in no small way. Tension builds in everyone as they climb the roller coaster's lift hill, in preparation for that terrifying first drop. Grizzly doesn't give them that terror, however. It sets its riders up with a beyond mild drop, and the slow turn usually has people thinking that this is going to be a real tame ride. The second drop, though, kicks them squarely in the jaw, with a wild hop that launches everyone out of their seat, and an evil tunnel that you just *know* the train is too big to fit into (there's also more action in the tunnel). The ride does this again and again, right to the end, and no one arrives back in the station without thinking how they were just completely bamboozled. Grizzly used to be completely enclosed in the woods, which made for an incredible night ride, and also allowed the ride's configuration to be totally cloaked. Park expansion opened the ride up, but somehow didn't remove the impact, just the mystery.

After your Grizzly ride, you'll be heading back to the Eiffel Tower. From there, you'll be able to access almost every portion of the park, and it's time to slow down.

Standing by the fountain, facing the Eiffel Tower, you'll find the park's remarkable kids area to your left. There are actually two adjacent areas: Nickelodeon Central and KidZville. Nickelodeon Central is home to some wet and wild fun and games, although the Green Slime you'll encounter is actually water (in most cases!). KidZville is home to rides that parents and children can enjoy together, including Scooby Doo's Ghoster Coaster, the park's fourth wooden device, and actually a totally fun ride for any age. KidZville's Town Square is the location of the smallest tyke rides and attractions, which parents will have to watch rather than experience with their kids. All in all, the three areas create the best selection of attractions for children in any park, anywhere (rivaled only by sister park Paramount's Kings Island and its similar selection). You could spend all day with your kids here and never see the rest of the park!

If you'd like to get wet (without a visit to the water park), the park offers three water rides. Diamond Falls is located near the Congo section—it's a shoot-the-chutes ride that offers a huge splash and a tunnel finale. The Shenandoah Log Flume is a fun-filled river journey in a cut out log—it's located in the Old Virginia section, near the Grizzly. There's also a rapids ride near the flume that has often been referred to as one of the best in the country.

The park prides itself on providing guests with entertainment featuring extremely talented performers, so be sure to take in a show or two, and don't miss the street characters throughout the park—they're based on Paramount movie characters. You'll also find Blue, Jimmy Neutron—Boy Genius, the Rugrats, Dora The Explorer, and many others in the kids areas.

You might also want to check out the food here. Pricing, believe it or not, is not as high as, say, a Disney or Six Flags park, and quality has always been a step higher. Snack items have been known to be mouthwatering, so you'll want to partake in at least a bit of the park's food offerings.

As dusk falls, plan to be near International Street. The huge fountain, alive with changing water sprays, suddenly becomes even more elaborate, as a dazzling light program begins as well. This would be a good time to journey to the top of the park's landmark Eiffel Tower as well. Both the fountain and the Tower are signature park attractions, and you don't want to miss the opportunity to relish their simple beauty. The Tower also offers incredible views of the park, and although you know you're not too far from civilization, you'll be challenged to see much of it beyond the park boundaries, even from this incredible vantage point.

Spend the evening, and, in fact, end it enjoying the park's three wooden coasters. All three pick up incredible amounts of speed this late in the day, and the lines for all cut down in length considerably. In fact, the park is happy to allow you to stay on the ride if there's no one waiting for your seat, and you may just be able to marathon on the wooden coaster of your choice if you're willing to remain at the same ride 'til the park closing time.

To end your day (and to delay your exit from this magical place), plan to get a snack, or shop on International Street. All the venues here remain open past park closing time, and the offerings range from park souvenirs to gift items to sports merchandise. You might be tempted to spend a few bucks here, and you won't be unhappy about it, either.

Leaving the parking lot can be difficult, as there is only one exit road, which leads onto a small access road outside the park. There are always traffic jams, unless you just stay in the park on International Street 'til they practically have to ask you to leave. Why sit in traffic when you can be sitting by a multi-colored lighted fountain, licking an ice cream cone?

SIX FLAGS OVER GEORGIA

275 Riverside Parkway
Austell, Georgia 30168
770-948-9290
www.sixflags.com
Admission: $40
Operating Schedule: Late March through Halloween. Park opens at
    10 A.M., with closing times 6 P.M. through 11 P.M., depending on time
    of season.

Park History

This was the second park built by the Six Flags Corporation, and made its debut in 1967. It's now considered one of the country's original theme parks, and while expansion has yielded some terrific new rides and attractions, at heart, there's still an inescapable down-home Southern charm throughout the park. Themed areas mix Old Georgia with today's super hero adventures, and for the most part, the park's original theme and layout remain untouched.

Major Attractions

Superman Ultimate Flight—Steel flying coaster
Georgia Cyclone—Wooden coaster based on Coney Island's
    Cyclone

Mind Bender—Classic steel looping coaster
Acrophobia—Stand up freefall tower
Great American Scream Machine—Classic wooden coaster

Getting There

Take I-20 West from Atlanta, and exit at Six Flags. The park is next to the interstate.

Planning to Go

A Six Flags season pass is essential. Discounts and coupons from fast food outlets may be in effect at the time of your visit, so call the park to find out exactly what is available.

The park is easy to enjoy on weekends (especially Sunday) early in the season, although opening day, depending on the weather, could be packed. Try to avoid Saturdays in the summer.

Beginning Your Day

Plan to arrive between 9:30 A.M. and park opening. When you enter the parking lot, you'll be driving right past the main entrance to the park, so if you have a large group, you may want to drop them off there so you won't have as much trouble getting from the car to the park. The parking lot is huge and stretches around the park. There used to be a back entrance to the park, which has been removed, so no matter where your car is parked, you'll have to return to the main entrance area, and it could be a long walk/tram ride away.

The main entrance to the park, upgraded in the late 1990s, is known as The Promenade. The area is basically a courtyard filled with shops and restaurants. It's a great place to gather and plan your day, and if you did indeed drop off members of your group before proceeding to park your car, you can meet up with them here.

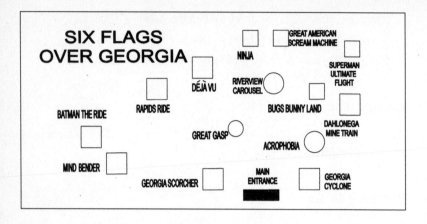

The layout of the park is not the easiest to traverse. You'll be encountering plenty of hills, dead ends, and downright confusing pathways. The park map provided with entry is an essential tool; make sure to pick up a few extras so every member of your group has one.

In the Park

At the end of the main entrance Promenade section, you'll either have to go left or right to venture further into the park. Go right into the British section, and head towards your first wake-up call of the day, the Georgia Cyclone. This is a wooden coaster inspired by the original Coney Island Cyclone, with steep drops and wicked twists. This version (there are currently three other Cyclone copies in the United States) is hailed as the best of the lot, and is considered by some to be even better than the original. It's a ferocious ride, and hopping on board first thing in the morning will wake you up better than a cup of coffee. It will not jar you beyond recognition, however, since a ride this early in the day will be a bit more sedate than one later on (the ride, like you, is just waking up!).

After you've cycloned, continue walking through the British area, passing under the park's railroad trestle, into the Confederate section. To your left, at the top of the small hill, is Acrophobia, a stand-

The USA's only stand-up, free fall drop tower, Acrophobia, at Six Flags Over Georgia. (*Credit: Frank De Santis*)

up freefall ride. Check to see if the line for this has reached monumental proportions—if not, hop on board for the plunge. If the Cyclone hadn't succeeded in waking you, this fall from 200 feet certainly will. Follow Acrophobia by hopping aboard Skybuckets, a cable car ride that will transport you to the Lickskillet section, and the back of the park.

When you've disembarked the sky ride, check to see if the huge inverted boomerang coaster, Déjà Vu, is operating (it's a prototype, and has limited operations). If so, hop on for a spin (you might not get another chance at this one, so you'll have to ride it when you see it running). Then, head for the Cotton States section, which are to your left when exiting Déjà Vu. You'll pass through the rustic shops of Lickskillet, and emerge into a red, white and blue world, where the wooden beauty Great American Scream Machine resides. Wander past the patriotically decorated entrance for that ride and continue to the back of the section—your first objective here is Superman Ultimate Flight, a steel "flying" coaster. This ride is just the latest in high-tech roller coaster riding, and features vehicles that hang passengers in a head-first flying position, dangling below the tracks, on a soaring, twisting flight through two inversions and an underground tunnel, all with amazing comfort and grace. The loading procedure on this is a bit longer than for other rides, so be prepared for it (a shoulder harness, a stomach brace, and leg restraints are involved, and all must be adjusted and checked before the train is dispatched).

After you've flown, head back through Cotton States, and catch the more traditional experience that is Great American Scream Machine. This wooden creation was built in 1972, and helped spur a renaissance of wooden coasters at large theme parks. It was actually one of the world's tallest in those days (a now almost diminutive 105 feet at its apex), but this is now considered a "family" coaster. While not all that gentle, it certainly doesn't reach the level of thrills found across the park on the more rambunctious Georgia Cyclone. Feel free to enjoy this grand coaster experience until the line starts to build.

Head back through Cotton States and Lickskillet, just past Déjà Vu and Skybuckets, hang a left, and proceed under the railroad trestle. Keep to the right through one corner of the French section, into the USA section, and just past the Looney Tunes Shop. Then,

make a right turn and head on down the hill into the Gotham City
area, where two more adventures await, one of which is one of the
best steel coasters on planet Earth.

At the very end of Gotham City resides a version of Six Flags's
signature ride (Batman The Ride). This inverted, outside-looping
coaster is one of the world's most intense coaster experiences, as it
flips through five different inversions all while dangling passengers
in ski-lift style seating. Batman The Ride exists at nearly every
major Six Flags theme park, in exactly the same configuration, so if
other Six Flags parks are in your travel plans, you'll only need to
hop on this one as time allows.

Right across the way, however, is a ride you'll want to experience
over and over. Mind Bender, a glorious steel ride built in the late
1970s, is a double-looping coaster that relies on true ups and downs
instead of multiple upside downs, all without need for more than a
traditional lap bar. Not only is the ride built on a hillside, and therefore able to have large drops throughout the course, but it also features two vertical 360-degree loops and one "horizontal" loop,
which is essentially a mind-numbing, steeply pitched helix. It's one
of the greats in the world of coastering. Ride as much as time
allows.

When you climb up the hill that leads out of Gotham City and
into USA, stay to the right, which will eventually lead you to the
covered arbor, and down the hill into the Georgia section. Here,
the main ride experience is Georgia Scorcher, a smooth as silk
stand-up coaster. In theory, most guests have already made their
way further into the park (Scorcher is one of the first rides encoun-
tered inside the main gate), so the line shouldn't be too long. You'll
probably only want one ride on this device anyway, and be prepared
for a longer load time (the vehicles must be height adjusted for each
oncoming passenger). Scorcher flings riders through a loop and
corkscrew and a few daunting twists and turns, all while in a totally
vertical standing position (a bicycle seat keeps passengers upright).

If you continue down the hill from Scorcher, you'll arrive back at
The Promenade, your starting point. It's now time to enjoy the

scenic beauty of the park and some of the more sedate offerings. Continue back into the British section, and walk through to the Confederate area.

This land of the Old South features a depot for the park's train, a major tool in circumnavigating the park, and the station for Dahlonega Mine Train, one of the most popular rides in the entire park. This is a family-style runaway train steel coaster, but with enough oomph to give even the heartiest thrill seeker a rush. The track stays close to the ground, and the run over rolling terrain, complete with quick turns and sudden drops, is actually quite hilarious. This is a great night ride, but is fun to ride any time of the day, and even long lines move quickly when multi-train operation is in effect.

Right next door to the mine train is the park's children's area—themed to Looney Tunes characters of course, but also with a Spanish flavor. You won't find an excessive amount of kiddie rides here, since the park has opted to go low on ride amounts and heavy on theming. It won't matter in the least to a child who's ready to ride. This might be the only area where the park fails miserably—there are just not enough kids rides here, not by a long shot.

The adjacent French section has one major attraction geared to families. It's a boat ride through the dark, known for years as Monster Plantation. This hilarious themed journey through a southern mansion and the swampy adjacent bayou may just be a Scooby Doo ride by the time you read this. In either case, it's a great ride for all, although smaller children have been known to quiver.

Next, comes the USA section, and the main ride here not to miss is Great Gasp. This was actually the first modern version of the Coney Island Parachute Drop, and in those days, it also operated like the original, offering a free falling drop from 200 feet with only a parachute to slow you down. These days, it's a completely controlled computerized descent, but that's just fine, too. It still manages to thrill.

Take a short stroll back through France, and head over the footpaths to the hilly peak at dead center of the park, which is where the famed Riverview Carousel proudly stands. This historic landmark is a restoration of the original Chicago, Illinois Riverview Park carousel, saved, refurbished, and moved to Six Flags after that famous park's demise in 1968. Six Flags was even thoughtful enough to duplicate the carousel building that housed the original, and the entire installation, on the hillside with benches placed around it, will make you want to just hang out and relax up there, watching the beautiful horses make their way around the course. On a lower level of the hill sits the Hanson Cars, an antique auto ride that is suitable for all family members. This spot in the park, with two rides that have wide appeal, is one of the nicest areas of any park anywhere, and a great spot to get away from the hustle and bustle of a theme park. You might want to stay up on this hill for a while, especially if the park is crowded.

As evening approaches, this charming park becomes a beautiful, twinkling wonderland. There are two great places to end your evening to choose from.

The first option is Cotton States, home of the Great American Scream Machine and Superman Ultimate Flight. Because these rides are furthest away from the main gate, this area of the park loses the majority of its crowds first. If you feel compelled to ride 'til the bitter end, Scream Machine might be the ride for you.

You could also choose Gotham City. This area is also a dead end in the park, and with both Batman The Ride and Mind Bender awaiting, is a great place to end the evening. Mind Bender is an incredible night ride experience. Gotham City is located quite a bit closer to the main entrance than Cotton States, but people on the way out of the park don't necessarily think to head back here, since strong rides are also located on either side of the main entrance (both lines for said rides, Georgia Scorcher and Georgia Cyclone, will probably be long right up 'til park closing).

A word of warning about closing time at this park: although the park claims to not have this policy, expect ride lines to close prior to the announced park closing time, so that the ride itself closes about when the park does (on busy nights, they'll cut lines on the more popular rides about forty-five minutes prior to closing). You won't be able to get in line for a ride right at closing, like most other parks allow.

What you will want to do, however, is linger in the park's shops and restaurants near the main gate as long as humanly possible. There will be a serious traffic jam getting out of the park and onto the highway, and you'd much rather be spending time sipping a mint julep (or barring that, a cold soda), wouldn't you?

SIX FLAGS OVER TEXAS

2201 Road To Six Flags
Arlington, Texas 76010
817-530-6000
www.sixflags.com
Admission: $40
Operating Schedule: Early March through Halloween. 10 A.M. opening, with closing times varying throughout the season. The park is also open late November through December for Holiday in the Park, with many park rides available.

Park History

This is the park responsible for theme parks as we know them today. Opening in 1961, the park combined the types of attractions found in Disneyland with the thrill rides found in traditional-style amusement parks. It also offered the first pay-one-price in the nation, a pricing policy now standard within the industry. Rides invented at Six Flags, such as the log flume (first operated here) and the full-sized tubular steel roller coaster (also a world's first for this park), have become staples at all the world's theme parks today. While much of the original park has given way to huge thrill rides, Six Flags Over Texas maintains itself as one of the best theme parks in the world.

Major Attractions

    Texas Giant—Huge wooden coaster

    Titan—Giant non-looping steel coaster

    Shockwave—Double-looping steel coaster

    Texas Chute Out—Parachute drop

    Mr. Freeze—Linear induction motor-launching steel shuttle looper

    Batman The Ride—Steel outside-looping inverted coaster

    Judge Roy Scream—Family wooden coaster

Getting There

Located midway between Dallas and Fort Worth, Texas. Take I-30 from either city, to Highway 360/Angus Wynne, Jr. Freeway, and follow the signs to the park entrance. The park is located right by the interstate.

Planning to Go

A Six Flags season pass is essential. Coupons for discounts may be available through Coca-Cola, or fast food outlets, so call the park to find out which are in effect at the time of your visit.

    The park is quite accessible on weekends early in the season, and September weekends as well. If you don't mind being a little chilly, the park's annual Christmas festival is also a great time to get a few rides in, although not all the rides in the park are available (water rides especially).

Beginning Your Day

As you enter the parking lot driveway, you'll drive right past the main gate of the park, so it would be a good idea to drop off your group there before heading through the parking tolls (so only one

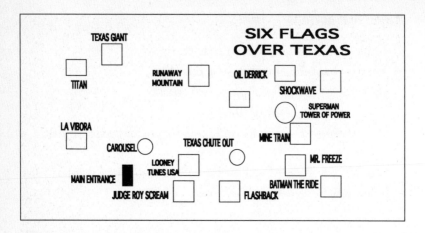

person has to walk any distance). Conveniently, the park's Looney Tunes USA kids area is located directly to the right of the main gate, so if you're travelling with small kids, you won't have to hunt their rides down. This is a big park, but it's also mostly flat, so walking is fairly easy.

In the Park

Once you've entered the park through the main gate, you'll be face to face with the park's beautiful Silver Star Carousel. This gorgeous machine, fully restored by the park, can be ridden at any time of the day without waiting too long, so save it for when you need a relaxing moment, and turn right, walking down the midway past Looney Tunes USA (on your right) and France (to your left). You're headed for the Boomtown section, and when you reach the crossroads, turn right and swing a left into Gotham City. This area contains two of the park's major thrill machines. First up is Mr. Freeze, a 225-foot-tall linear induction motor-launching coaster, which travels through a high speed inversion and high banked turn, then zips up a 90 degree spike, at which time it falls backwards through the circuit. The ride is very intense, to say the least. At the very end of Gotham is Six Flags' signature ride, Batman The Ride, an inverted, outside-

Mr. Freeze, an ultimate thriller. (*Credit: Six Flags Over Texas*)

looping coaster with riders in ski lift-style seating. This is also a heavy duty thrill ride, with non-stop pacing.

With two of the park's more relentless rides out of the way, leave Gotham and head straight into Good Times Square, a 50s-themed section that contains the Texas Chute Out, a semi-thrilling parachute drop ride, and Flashback, a boomerang coaster (the most-sold production model in the amusement industry—only ride it here if you've beaten the crowds to it). Near the Chute Out is a tunnel leading to Judge Roy Scream, the park's family wooden coaster. This fun little ride doesn't offer huge thrills, but serves up hill after hill of consistent speed, relying on fun rather than fright to deliver the goods. It's the perfect ride for young and old.

Now, head back through Good Times Square, and make a left back into Boomtown. This is the park's western themed section, and the first must-ride here is Runaway Mine Train. This was the first ride of its kind in the world, and features more twists, turns, and dips than you'd normally expect from a family ride. This one is just plain fun, suitable for all, and you might want to ride a few times, just for the laughs.

Continuing along, you'll eventually reach the Tower section, home to the huge Oil Derrick observation tower, which is a must-ride, but at any time of the day (it normally has no line). Turn right at the Tower, cross the train tracks, and venture toward the double-looping steel monster ahead. This is Shockwave, a marvel of a classic steelie that offers a 116-foot climb, two back to back, very intense loops, and pure roller coaster thereafter. The design is so precise, passengers ride without the need of shoulder harnesses—a simple lap bar is all that's necessary to hold you in place. Since the ride is a bit off the beaten path, ride several times before you venture back to the main midway. You'll be glad you did.

Heading back to the Tower, veer right, and follow the path around into the Texas section. On your left, look for a small path that leads to Runaway Mountain and its enclosed steel coaster, totally in the dark. If the line hasn't built up for this yet, hop on. Make no mistake—this is a small ride, but without benefit of lights, it seems huge, and it's filled with disorienting twists and turns, so you're never quite sure how high you are or how deep your drop is. If you were to see the ride outdoors, you'd be amazed at how tiny it appears.

Back on the path to the Texas Section, you'll head for the park's two major rides: Texas Giant, the wooden monster, and Titan, the steel giant.

Since its 1990 debut, the Texas Giant has held the #1 wooden coaster spot on many lists, and to this day is still considered the "masterpiece of mayhem." It begins with a 143-foot climb, and the 138-foot drop that follows leads to a breathless series of relentless hills and turns, so non-stop that riders don't even get a chance to catch their breaths. This terror ends with a series of small dips that encircle the entire main structure of the ride, and are taken with such fury that when the train comes to a stop in the station, passengers are still screaming.

Right next to the entrance to the Giant is the path leading to the park's latest coaster thrill ride, Titan. This is a steel, non-looping ride, with a massive 255-foot-tall first drop. Like its wooden neighbor, it has a relentless pace with non-stop speed and action 'til the very end. Gotham City may be across the park, but the *real* Dynamic Duo resides right here, in the Texas section.

If you'd like, right next to this pair of mighty muscle machines is the park's log flume. While it's not incredibly wet or terribly exciting, ride it for the pure historical significance, since this was the world's very first log flume—a ride which has now become a theme park tradition.

Continuing into the Mexican section, you'll see a huge, twisting, serpent-like trough ride with individual cars zooming through it. This is La Vibora (The Viper), a bobsled-style ride that is very suitable for the entire family. A limited amount of vehicles on the ride may lead to a very long, slow-moving line, so check to see how long the queue is, and bypass it if it seems to be too long a wait—you can ride this later if you need to.

You'll find yourself back at the Silver Star Carousel after you exit Mexico, and it's time to take a slower journey around the park now to catch some of the other delightful and thrilling attractions the park has to offer. Now might be a good time to take a spin on the Silver Star, one of the nation's premier carousels. It will not only give you a break from thrill rides, but will allow your heartbeat to slow down. Enjoy this classic amusement park ride to its fullest, since more thrills await.

The nearby Looney Tunes USA section is the park's kiddie land. Filled with smaller versions of adult rides, it's also one of the more conveniently located kids areas in a major theme park. You can drop off kids (with an adult chaperone) here and do the first round of the park and pick them up on your second round. They should have had plenty of time to do all the rides and attractions within the area by the time you return, and the nearby Looney Tunes Shop could soak up even more time. It's filled with Looney Tunes merchandise of all types, and kids (and parents alike, for that matter) are bound to find something they want to bring home with them.

Just ahead, on the right, is Splash Water Falls, the park's shoot-the-chute ride. This isn't much of a ride; its sole purpose is to soak riders. A twenty-passenger boat climbs a fifty-foot hill, turns, and dives into a pool below, creating a huge tidal wave that drenches passengers. Only ride this one-note attraction if it doesn't have a line.

The skeletal tower just past Splash Water is the Wildcatter. Once known as the Texas Cliffhanger, this was part of the first generation of freefall rides. A four passenger cabin is lifted to 120 feet and then dropped down a shaft, with passengers coming to a halt lying on their backs. It's brief but extremely intense.

Turn left at the midway intersection and head to the Oil Derrick now. This 300-foot-tall observation tower is a park landmark, and the views of not only the park but the entire Dallas/Fort Worth metropolis are breathtaking. You'll want to stay up at the top for a while, especially if it's a hot day, since the breezes up here are wonderfully soothing.

Heading into the Texas section again, there are two great family rides. The wonderful antique cars are park classics, cars that you can drive and steer, but on a track guide to help even the littlest motorists reach their destination. The Yosemite Sam is a dark boat ride that takes guests and puts them, literally, in the middle of a cartoon, complete with amazing animatronics of all your favorite Looney Tunes characters. Kids and parents alike will enjoy this one.

There's also a station for the park's railroad, always a good choice for transportation around the park, or just a relaxing journey (many guests like to return to their starting off point, even though there are stations located elsewhere in the park).

Food at the park is the usual fare for the usual prices, but one thing you must try while in the park is a "Pink Thing," which is an ice cream bar, pink of course. It's a park tradition (and not all that bad, either).

As dusk approaches, you'll need to make a choice. There are two areas you'll want to be in—either Gotham City/Good Times Square, or Texas. The former will offer more ride choices (Mr. Freeze, Batman The Ride, Judge Roy Scream, Flashback, and Texas Chute

Out), but the latter will feature the two main attractions in the park (Texas Giant and Titan). Undoubtedly, lines will be longer for Giant and Titan than for the rides in Gotham/Goodtimes, but there are those times when you'll have to make the choice between quality and quantity, and this is one of them. Night rides on Texas Giant are incredible, however, if that helps you decide.

Leaving the park at closing is usually not much of a problem, as the parking lot has several exit gates, and while the traffic eventually all leads to the interstate, not having a bottleneck at one exit certainly helps keep things moving. You'll be relieved that the ending of your day was as pleasurable as the rest of it.

Note: If visiting during Holiday in the Park, certain rides will not be available, such as all water rides, Texas Chute Out, and Oil Derrick (the last two are decorated for the holidays). Various other rides and attractions will also be unavailable, but all major rides will be open. Check with the park to make sure that nothing is closed for winter maintenance (Texas Giant has been known to sleep during Holiday in the Park).

UNIVERSAL STUDIOS ORLANDO

1000 Universal Studios Plaza
Orlando, Florida 32819
407-363-8000
www.universalstudiosescape.com
Admission: $50
Operating Schedule: Open daily, year round at 9 A.M. (closing times vary)

Park History

Universal Studios Florida opened in 1990 as central Florida's answer to Universal's popular Hollywood theme park/movie studio, and to cash in on the gazillions of people already visiting the area because of the famed Disney parks nearby. The park quickly caught on and became one of the highest attended parks in the country, its "Ride The Movies" slogan acting like a magnet to pull guests through the front gate. In 1999, the park was joined by Islands of Adventure, a full-fledged thrill ride theme park. Both parks are adjacent to Universal City Walk, an area of restaurants and shops. Universal Orlando (which is what both parks together are called) is perhaps the one single entity that gives Disney a run for its money in central Florida.

Major Attractions

In Universal Studios Florida
> Back to the Future—Car ride simulator
> Twister—Simulated encounter with a tornado
> Terminator 2: 3-D—Combination live action and motion
>   picture adventure

In Islands of Adventure
> The Incredible Hulk—Steel looping coaster
> Dueling Dragons—Twin-track inverted outside-looping coaster
> The Amazing Adventures of Spider-Man—Dark ride adventure

Getting There

Take I-4 to exit 75A, Universal Boulevard.

Planning to Go

Universal Studios Florida and Islands of Adventure are located right in theme park central, competing with Disney parks nearby and two different Busch Entertainment Corporation parks. It's doubtful that you're just going to be visiting Universal, so check with your travel agent about packages that might be available to save admission dollars for all area theme parks. One that you might want to check on is the Orlando Flex Ticket, which allows admission to both Universal Parks, Seaworld, Wet and Wild, and Busch Gardens Tampa Bay.

The parks tend to be far less crowded during winter months, but also tend to have a much earlier closing time (7 P.M. in some cases), which won't leave you much time to get everything done if it turns out that the day you go does wind up being crowded. It's almost best to plan your visit to Orlando when the parks are open late (and remember, they don't *want* you to get on every ride in Orlando; they want you to spend days at the parks, so they limit the hours of operation, forcing you to have to come back). Both Universal Parks are not huge in acreage, nor do they have tremendous amounts of attractions. Still, you'll never be able to do all there is to do at either park in one day, and that's just the way they like it.

That said, do not even think about planning a visit to both Universal parks in one day. You'll only scratch the surface of each, and it will be one of the most expensive days you'll ever spend *not* going on rides and attractions! This is a two-day adventure.

Beginning Your Day

Orlando is a bustling tourist community, one that awakens early, as the theme parks all begin operation as early as 9 A.M. (with even earlier times for resort hotel guests). Plan on lots of traffic getting to the Universal parking garages—in fact, no matter where you're staying, leave about an hour's worth of travel time. An early arrival will still afford you enough time to do the park, but a late arrival will cut back on your time, and you definitely want as many hours in the park as you can get. Choosing a rainy day (if you have the luxury of doing so) might be the best bet you have.

In the Park

Universal Studios Florida

You'll be amazed at how small in acreage this park really is, although you'll probably spend the entire day attempting to do all you want to do. When you enter the park, you'll be on an avenue of shops, so bypass them and head straight down the midway to Twister, located on the left almost near the end of the street. This

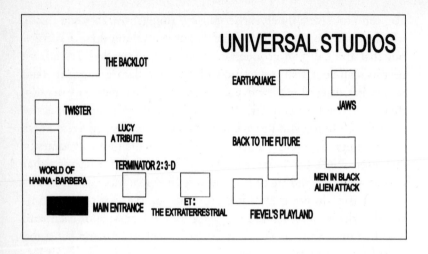

attraction is based on the disaster movie of the same name, and it is a very realistic depiction of an encounter with a tornado. Wind and sound effects are very strong, and might make some guests uncomfortable (but hey, it's only a movie, ummm, theme park attraction!).

Leaving Twister, head straight for the lake, and when you get to it, veer left. On your left is Earthquake, another realistic attraction, which puts you smack dab in a tremor while riding a Los Angeles subway car. This one is more fun than terrifying, although if you're from California, you won't find it very funny. Next door is Jaws, a boat ride through a New England fishing village where that nasty shark might just pay a visit (he does, several times). The possibility of getting wet exists on this ride—the shark is big, and he likes to rock the boat!

Next up is Men in Black Alien Attack, an interactive attraction where passengers, armed with raygun zappers, hunt down alien creatures in the streets of New York City. There are multiple endings to the ride, depending on how many shots reach their targets. A great attraction, with great special effects.

Continuing clockwise around the lake, you'll see the huge building that houses Back to the Future The Ride. This is a marvel of a simulator, all the more realistic because each group of eight passengers gets to sit in their own DeLorean, which lifts up out of a docking bay and seems to fly in front of a huge movie screen. You'll hardly notice the dozens of other vehicles also enjoying the flight. Note: This is a very turbulent ride. Insist that you sit in the front row of the car, or else you'll spend the entire ride banging your head against the back headrest, which will go a long way toward ruining your day.

Still travelling clockwise around the lake, you'll encounter a fork in the street. Take the left path, which will lead you to Terminator 2: 3-D, a 3-D movie, live action, fourth dimension attraction that will amaze you at every turn. It features a movie based on the Terminator series, live actors that seem to come right out of the screen and into the theatre, fog effects, seat motion, and surround screens. This is one of the best attractions to be found at any park in the world. You won't believe how totally assaulted your senses will be.

For more leisurely fun in the park, choose the Lucy exhibit (near the front gate). Based on Lucille Ball's fabulous career, the exhibit contains *I Love Lucy* clips, scrap books, personal items from Ms. Ball's collection, and more. If you're a fan of the wacky redhead (and who isn't?), you'll love visiting her virtual museum.

For children, Fievel's Playland, Barney, and Animal Actors are all adjacent (near Back to the Future), and offer play areas that feature some of the best loved kids characters existing today. Of course, E.T. Adventure, with passengers riding on flying bicycles, is also full of charm for young and old alike (best done near closing time, when lines are at their shortest). Also of note is The Funtastic World of Hanna-Barbera, a rocket ship journey with Yogi Bear and Boo Boo where guests help save the kidnapped Elroy Jetson.

The park offers various shows that are movie stunt related, and the theming throughout is so gorgeous it's a pleasure just to walk around and soak up the atmosphere. This is a great park for people who love theme parks, but don't appreciate the more rambunctious, traditional rides they offer.

Islands of Adventure

If you *are* looking for a more traditional theme park experience, however, right next to Universal Studios Florida is this new theme

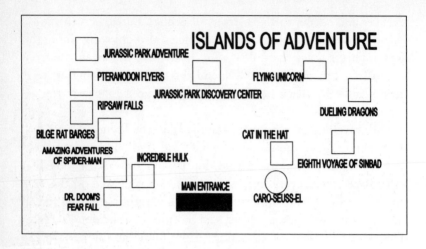

park, a fantasy world that features the classic thrill rides we know and love.

The park is laid out in a circular pattern around a central lagoon, with one single circular midway. There's very little way to circumnavigate the park other than to just hop on attractions as you come to them. Guests might tend to head left, to the Incredible Hulk coaster right inside the main gate, and we'll follow them, but then change directions quickly.

As you enter the Port of Entry, you'll see the huge green looping coaster known as Incredible Hulk to your left. This is a coaster that launches you up to the highest point, where you're flipped head over heels into an inversion before diving back to earth. More flips, twists, and inversions come at a rapid pace. This huge green machine is a landmark in the Marvel Super Hero Island section. Also in Super Hero Island is perhaps the best dark ride adventure in the world, the Amazing Adventures of Spider-Man. This 3-D ride through offers incredible effects, and combines stunning visuals and very real physical motion.

Once you've attacked these two main attractions early after your arrival, head back into the Port of Entry and enter Seuss Landing. You'll now be travelling counterclockwise around the park.

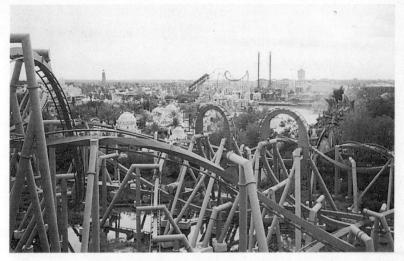

The gnarled, twisted track of Dueling Dragons. (*Credit: Frank De Santis*)

Within Seuss Landing, Dr. Seuss characters come to life. On Cat in the Hat, a dark ride adventure, you'll ride couches through the world of this famous feline, complete with a visit from Thing One and Thing Two. The area is also home to the Caro-Seuss-el, one of the more fantastical carousels you'll ever behold, with Dr. Seuss characters to ride instead of the more traditional horses. You'll even find a One Fish, Two Fish, Red Fish, Blue Fish attraction in this magical land.

The main attraction in the next section, The Lost Continent, is Dueling Dragons, a huge red and blue dual-track inverted coaster, with passengers riding ski-lift style seats that hang from the track above. At times, both tracks head toward each other, and the feet of the passengers on opposing trains come within a few feet of each other (a very unusual and daunting visual). For a less adventurous coaster experience, there's the Flying Unicorn, a family coaster with gentle dips and turns.

Moving right along to the Jurassic Park section, enjoy an educational visit to the Jurassic Park Discovery Center, a replica of the movie's main attraction center, featuring games and exhibits where guests learn about the prehistoric giants that once roamed the earth. The major attraction in this section, however, is the Jurassic Park River Adventure. A boat ride, this attraction will make you feel as if you're visiting the real Jurassic Park from the movie. It's filled with animatronic dinosaurs and can be quite startling. The ride reaches its penultimate moment with an eighty-five-foot plunge down a watery trough, into darkness. Nearby is the Pteranodon Flyers, a gentle suspended coaster suitable for all family members (though adults might not be permitted to ride without a child).

Next is Toon Lagoon with its watery adventures. Dudley Do-Right's Ripsaw Falls is a heavily themed flume ride, with an incredible splashdown finale. This is *not* your everyday log flume. It's theming is so extravagant, you'll almost be tempted not to pay attention to the ride itself, and the design of the course is as incredible as the theming. The same goes for Popeye and Bluto's Bilge-Rat Barges, another heavily themed water adventure, this time a river raft ride taken to amazing extremes. Both rides not only present watery thrills, but they also tell a story featuring the title characters.

You'll eventually find yourself back in Marvel Super Heroes Island, where you started off your day. The design of the park screams for you to take another journey, this time hitting the attractions you bypassed on your first go round. Let's look at some of the more noteworthy ones you missed.

In Super Heroes Island, there's Storm Force Acceleration, a spinning tea cups ride with heavy theming, and Dr. Doom's Fear Fall, a ride that shoots passengers to the top of a 150-foot tower, and then forces them back to earth faster than force of gravity.

The Lost Continent is home to the Eight Voyages of Sinbad, an amazing adventure show in an open air stadium with death defying stunts.

Kids will love Camp Jurassic in Jurassic Park, as they explore this prehistoric playground, complete with "dinosaur" nets and mines.

And for the kid in all of us, there's *Me Ship, the Olive* located in Toon Lagoon, a charming reproduction of Popeye's vessel turned into a three-level interactive arcade.

Although expensive, you might want to check out some of the park's food outlets. In Seuss Landing, there's the Green Eggs and Ham Café, which is not to be missed (or believed). In Lost Continent, don't miss Mythos, a full service restaurant that is often voted as the best in-park dining establishment in the world.

Shopping in the park can be expensive, but the main store you should not miss is The Islands of Adventure Trading Company, featuring merchandise from all the lands found in the park. It's right in the Port of Entry section, and makes a good last stop before you head out.

Hopefully, the park is open late when you visit, so you'll be able to experience some of your favorite attractions a second or third time. Leaving this magical wonderland behind while it's still early won't leave you with the best feeling, as the park is so magical to behold, you'll feel as if you could stay for days. Well, that's the idea, isn't it?

7

THE WEST COAST

KNOTT'S BERRY FARM
PARAMOUNT'S GREAT AMERICA
SANTA CRUZ BEACH BOARDWALK
SIX FLAGS MAGIC MOUNTAIN
SIX FLAGS MARINE WORLD

KNOTT'S BERRY FARM

8039 Beach Boulevard
Buena Park, California 90620
714-220-5000
www.knotts.com
Admission: $42
Operating Schedule: Open daily (except Christmas) at 9 A.M. or 10 A.M.
   Closing times vary depending on season.

Park History

This park started as a real berry farm. A restaurant, still known as
Mrs. Knott's Chicken Dinner Restaurant, opened on the site, and
proved so popular that several western-themed attractions were
added to occupy the hundreds of people waiting to get into the
restaurant. Thus, Knott's Berry Farm, the theme park, was born (it

dates to 1940, a full fifteen years before Walt Disney opened his park a few blocks away). The park bills itself as the oldest operating theme park in the country, and was privately owned by the Knott's family until Cedar Fair, LP bought the park in the late 1990s and began turning it into a full-fledged resort. New, spectacular rides came with the purchase, and now Knott's holds its own in the competitive Southern California theme park market (and the country, for that matter). It's not only a great family park, but one that is also heavy on thrills. And while most parks that have been purchased by large corporate themers have lost much of their old-time charm, you can still see authentic Native American shows here, ride the stagecoach, and pan for gold, all attractions that date back to 1940, when this vast expanse of land was truly just a farm.

Major Attractions

Ghost Rider—Large wooden roller coaster

Xcelerator—200-foot-tall steel launching coaster

Perilous Plunge—Super tall and super steep shoot-the-chutes water ride

Supreme Scream—330-foot-tall freefall tower ride

Log Ride—One of the world's greatest log flumes

Getting There

Take I-91 to the Beach Boulevard exit. Head south five blocks from the interstate; the parking entrance is on the right. The tall rides are very visible from the interstate and the surrounding area.

Planning to Go

Knott's is one of the best examples of a well-rounded family park in the world. If you crave thrills, the park has a few of the best. If you have no intention of even thinking about boarding a ride, you'll have plenty to do throughout the park. More importantly, this is not a cartoon-character-laden place for kids; while the Peanuts characters *do* hold court here, there's also a bit of American history to be had, and adults will find enough to entertain them, as will the hardcore thrill seekers. Therefore, plan on bringing the entire family here, because everyone will love the place.

The park offers substantial discounts in a promotion with Coca-Cola. Call to find out exactly what type is in effect at the time of your planned visit. There's also an after 4 P.M. half-price ticket available, but that's not recommended, as you'll want as much time here as you can get. Southern California residents receive a bonus discount of $10 off the regular Admission price, so make sure you have identification if you live in that part of the state. Plan your visit during a weekday, and check to see when the park will have extended hours on those days.

Beginning Your Day

This is one of those parks that might distract you as you enter the parking lot. You'll pass by the California Marketplace, a thriving village of shops and restaurants right outside the main gate, and it's definitely a place you'll want to spend time in, especially if you're travelling with older adults who really don't want to try that huge roller coaster right next door. *But*, you'll have plenty of time for that later, so park your car and head right into the theme park. Make sure you arrive at the park no later than 8:45, so you'll not only get a good parking spot, but you'll be ready to enter the park promptly when they open at 9 A.M. (call to verify operating schedule the day of your visit—it is subject to change).

In the Park

Once inside the main gate, head to the left, because your first stop is going to be Ghost Rider, the huge wooden roller coaster that towers right next to the Marketplace. This ride is the longest

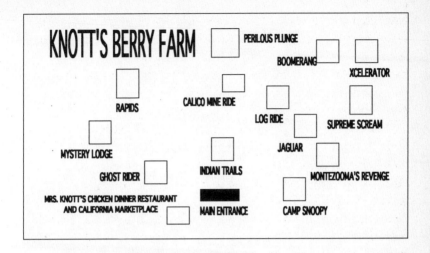

KNOTT'S BERRY FARM

PERILOUS PLUNGE

BOOMERANG

XCELERATOR

CALICO MINE RIDE

RAPIDS

LOG RIDE

SUPREME SCREAM

MYSTERY LODGE

JAGUAR

GHOST RIDER

INDIAN TRAILS

MONTEZOOMA'S REVENGE

MRS. KNOTT'S CHICKEN DINNER RESTAURANT
AND CALIFORNIA MARKETPLACE

MAIN ENTRANCE

CAMP SNOOPY

wooden coaster in the West, and one of the best. It will normally have long lines all day, as it is close to the entrance, and you'll need to get your ride in as soon as you enter the park. This is a wild ride, so be selective as to who in your group takes the challenge.

Once you're done with this wooden beauty, head back to the main gate and towards Fiesta Village. You'll pass through Indian Trails, under the stage coach trestle, and yes, you'll be captivated by what you see along the way, but keep going right to the Boardwalk section in the back of the park.

There are two roller coasters located here: Boomerang and Xcelerator. Boomerang is the standard issue back-and-forth inverting coaster, of which dozens and dozens exist worldwide, so ride it only if the line hasn't built up. Xcelerator, on the other hand, is a fiendish launching device with the world's steepest incline and first drop (both set at 90 degrees, straight up and down). While an intense ride, it's also very short, so you don't want to wait any considerable time for it. The funky vehicles are themed to 1950s hot rods, but don't think the "cute" aspect means anything at all—this is hardcore thrill riding. Then, immediately hop on Supreme Scream, if you dare. This intimidating 330-foot-tall freefall ride uses air compression to launch the vehicles faster than gravity allows.

The diabolical Ghost Rider wooden coaster. (*Credit: Knott's Berry Farm: © 2003 Knott's Berry Farm*)

Now, scoot over to the Log Ride, one of the best flumes in the world. It's heavily-themed, has aspects of a dark ride, and is just a fun experience for the entire family.

You're now a bit wet, but you have two major rides to conquer in Fiesta Village. Jaguar is a family coaster, a four-minute trip over the section's other Mexican-themed attractions, and while not wild, it's a fun-filled experience for everyone. Even Grandma can join her grandkids on this one, and you'll all be hooting and hollering. You'll notice that the Jaguar course zips right through the loop of the double spiked Montezooma's Revenge, the park's first shuttle looping launch coaster. This is a classic steel design, and while brief, the experience is very thrilling. This design was once prolific, but currently there are only two in operation in the United States, both in California.

Now, if you're travelling with small children, mosey into Camp Snoopy, the park's childrens area, which is so full of charm that even adults will want to spend a bit of time here. Older kids can actually enjoy a few of the spin-and-twist flat rides in Fiesta Village while the toddlers take a few spins on rides built just for them.

And now it's time to head back to the main gate. There, you'll have to make a choice, and neither of them involves riding of any type. If it's taken you a while to get on the rides you've just visited, and you're feeling it may be time to slow down and have lunch, head out the main gate exit (get your hand stamped for later read-mittance) and stroll on over to Mrs. Knott's Chicken Dinner Restaurant. This is the place that is responsible for this marvelous park's existence, and it really is the best chicken dinner you'll ever have. Pricing is not unreasonable, and you just won't want to miss the experience (nor will you want to miss a slice of boysenberry pie). After lunch, stroll through the shops of the Marketplace while your food digests; you'll be glad you did. An amazing selection of gift items, along with Knott's food products, awaits. There's also a park souvenir gift shop, so if you forget something while you're in the actual park, you can pick it up here as you leave for the day.

If you actually manage to accomplish all the above and still have time before lunch, then opt to visit the Indian Trails section of the park before you head to the Chicken Dinner Restaurant. It's located right inside the main gate, and is the original section of the park, containing attractions that were set up to entertain people waiting to get into the historic restaurant in its earlier years. This authentic section, containing many real historic mine town buildings (relo-cated to the park), will captivate you for a much longer time than you may think. There are also authentic Native Americans who par-ticipate in many exhibits, including real handcrafts, dances, and demonstrations of early Native American life. The park refers to this section as its heart and soul. It may just be the heart and soul of America in general, and you'll just want to get lost in the magic of it.

Whether you chose to do Indian Trails before or after lunch, wind your way over to Ghost Town (to the left of Indian Trails). There's more early American theming here, and again, you'll be fascinated. Past that, in Wild Water Wilderness, is a very special attraction, Mystery Lodge. It is a live-action show with special effects, and tells the tale of Old Storyteller, a Native American with magical powers. The show itself is powerful, with a simple beauty that even the hardest individual can't help but be touched by. Don't miss it. Next door to this section is Bigfoot Rapids, a family raft ride that is guaranteed to get passengers wet.

There are several other attractions that the entire family can do together. In Calico Square (the center of the park), there's the Calico Mine Ride, an in-the-dark train ride through an old-time Western mine, and the Calico Railroad, a outdoor large-gauge train ride that circles nearly the entire back half of the park. In Boardwalk, the Sky Cabin provides a bird's-eye view of the entire park without relying on thrills. Indian Trails offers an honest-to-goodness Stage Coach ride, and Fiesta Village is home to the park's carousel. Thrill seekers will enjoy the dozen or so spin-and-flip rides located throughout both Boardwalk and Fiesta Village.

As night falls, it would be a good plan to re-visit some of the main attractions in the park, starting with Xcelerator in the back of the park. Ghost Rider, near the main gate, will have a long line right up 'til closing, as people leaving the park will attempt to get one more ride in, but it's worth it.

The California Marketplace shops will fill up near park closing as well, since guests will be stopping to make last minute purchases. If you've forgotten to pick up an item, this is the time to get it. The Marketplace contains a shop devoted to Knott's Berry Farm park merchandise, some of which is unique.

And perhaps the best part of a visit to Knott's Berry Farm is that it's located right in town. You won't have an hours-long drive home, and you won't be in the middle of nowhere. If you're still raring to go, there's an entire city still very much open for your enjoyment.

PARAMOUNT'S GREAT AMERICA

4701 Great America Parkway
Santa Clara, California 95052
408-988-1776
www.pgathrills.com
Admission: $46
Operating Schedule: Late March through mid-October

Park History

The park opened in 1976 as one of two Marriott Great America
parks (the other one north of Chicago), each with the same rides
and layout, and part of a planned trio (the third park was never
built). When Marriott got out of the park business, the Chicago park
was purchased by Six Flags, while this California location was taken
by Kings Entertainment, operators of Kings Island. The park
became Paramount's Great America when the chain was purchased
by Paramount Pictures, and is now owned by Viacom, the huge multimedia giant that includes Paramount Pictures as one of its units.

Major Attractions

Stealth—Steel Flying Coaster
Top Gun—Steel inverted, outside-looping coaster
Vortex—Steel looping stand-up coaster
Drop Zone Stunt Tower—220-foot-tall freefall tower

Getting There

Take US 101 to the Great America Parkway exit.

Planning to Go

Tickets purchased in advance for this park are available at a $5 dis-
count (see the Paramount's Kings Island section for more on this

feature). The park bests the competition by also offering a season pass known as the WOW card for the full price of a daily Admission ticket. The WOW card doesn't offer the extended benefits (like free parking) that a season pass does, but if you plan to visit the park more than once, this is the way to go.

Beginning Your Day

The park's layout has the same problem that Six Flags Great America has (see that chapter for a description). But while the Six Flags park crammed in rides everywhere, and added an entire new section, this park maintained the same layout, did not expand in the park area at all (it's virtually land-locked by a surrounding office park), and kept truer to the original Marriott park than Six Flags did. Because of the single, circular midway, be prepared for some difficulty in maneuvering. The first thing you'll want to do when you arrive is take advantage of the WOW card policy, that offers an all season long Admission for the price of your single day ticket.

At press time, there is an energy crisis in California, so the park may open certain rides on a limited basis (currently, all the water-based rides in the park open at noon and close at dusk).

In the Park

When you enter the park through the main gate, you'll be in the Carousel Plaza section of the park, facing the entry plaza fountain, behind which stands the world's tallest double deck carousel, the Columbia. You'll be forced to either take a left or right turn at the carousel to journey further into the park, and this single-path midway is your only path through the entire park.

You'll want to turn right and head directly for Invertigo, the park's single-train, suspended inverted shuttle coaster, which is located across from the entrance to Demon, about halfway down the midway toward the back of the park. This is a boomerang-style shuttle coaster, similar to the most prominent coaster design in exis-

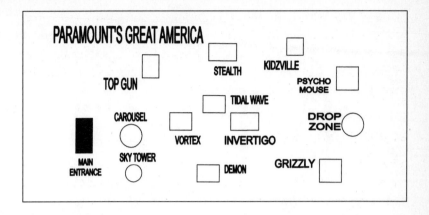

PARAMOUNT'S GREAT AMERICA

TOP GUN

STEALTH

KIDZVILLE

PSYCHO MOUSE

CAROUSEL

TIDAL WAVE

DROP ZONE

VORTEX

INVERTIGO

MAIN ENTRANCE

SKY TOWER

DEMON

GRIZZLY

tence, but has cars with ski-lift-style seating. Except for the front and back cars, each car faces another, so you'll be able to watch the expressions of two other riders during your journey (and they'll be able to watch yours, too). This provides half the fun of an Invertigo experience. Because of its single train operation, you'll want to get on it first thing, as a long line can mean a long wait.

After you've done this, continue to the back of the park and the extremely tall tower known as Drop Zone Stunt Tower. This is one of the world's tallest freefall rides, a towering 220 feet in the air, and features seats that dangle riders' legs above the ground. It's a brief but sensationally thrilling experience.

Continuing in a counterclockwise direction, to your right is Psycho Mouse, which appears to be a small family coaster. This is the modern version of those Wild Mouse rides that were invented in the 1950s, and features single cars that take wild, hairpin turns that make you feel like your car (and therefore, you) will go flying off the track into the midway below. While the ride is suitable for all family members, it might not be as mild as everyone would like, so it may be best to send a few test riders on to determine if all in your group can handle the experience. This style ride always surprises riders.

Still heading counterclockwise around the park, you'll encounter Stealth to your right, and Greezed Lightnin' to your left. Both are

Invertigo, a suspended boomerang. (*Credit: Frank De Santis*)

high-thrill experiences. On Greezed Lightnin', your single train will be catapulted into a loop, up a 70-degree tower, where it will lose momentum and simply drop back down into the loop backwards, race through the loading dock, and up another tower to slow it down, where it will then drop back into the station and be braked to a sudden stop. This ride debuted with the park in 1976, and is still one of the more intense rides around. Stealth, built in 2000, is a "flying" coaster, with passengers seated four-across in a lay-down position (your body will be roughly situated as if you are sitting, with knees bended). When you board, you'll be seated in a normal position, facing backwards on the track. The seats will tip backwards until you're lying on your back (still in the seated position), and the train will move head-first out of the station, and up the lift hill.

When you reach the top, the track will do a 360-degree spiral that will send you flying face-down into the first drop, and through many of the upcoming maneuvers. At times, the track will spiral you onto your back again, and will execute corkscrews and loops. This is a very thrilling ride, needless to say.

Make your way to the front of the park, where the station for the Delta Flyer sky ride is located, and hop on board. You're now going to tour the park again and catch the attractions you didn't do before, at a much more leisurely pace.

When you disembark from the sky ride at the other end of the park, head toward the Drop Zone tower (you're now travelling clockwise around the park), and the Grizzly wooden coaster. This is a very mild, family-oriented woodie, suitable for all, so no one need be intimidated. For the smoothest ride, select only the odd-numbered seats throughout the train. You may notice beneath and surrounding the Grizzly resides an antique car ride, Barney Oldfield Speedway. This is a tracked, drive-and-steer-it-yourself ride that all family members can enjoy together.

The thrills return on Demon, a double-looping, double-corkscrew steel coaster with an interesting history. The ride originally opened in the late 1970s as Turn of the Century and featured normal up and down hills, climaxing at the end with the double corkscrew. The hills were eventually removed and replaced by the double-loop element, and the ride was given its new, more menacing name. Since today's looping coasters are far more extravagant and thrilling, Demon could almost be considered a mild-mannered looper, so it may be suitable for more members of your group.

The last big ride you'll encounter as you make your way back to the front of the park is Vortex, an extremely smooth stand-up coaster, located on the right of the midway. The ride features two inversions (a 360-degree loop and a corkscrew), and numerous twists and turns, all executed while passengers are in a standing position.

Leaving Vortex, stroll past the Columbia Carousel and front entrance again, and continue your clockwise journey. Directly ahead is Top Gun, a steel inverted coaster, featuring ski-lift-style seating with legs dangling. This ride had to be squeezed into a relatively small space, so at one point it travels over one of the park's theaters, and finishes its twists and dives directly over a lake (and quite nearly allows rider's feet to walk on the surface of the water). This is a thrilling ride, but not so thrilling as to be off-limits to only the hardcore thrill seekers. Give it a test run.

Following the clockwise pattern again, you'll almost walk under the path the Delta Flyer sky ride takes to the other side of the park. Near the entrance to Greezed Lightnin' is the Paramount Action FX Theater, which is currently showing two different attractions with moving seats that coincide with the action on the screen. This type of attraction can be suitable for all, as the motion is not extreme, and the theatres come equipped with non-moving benches for those who really can't decide if they want the enhanced experience.

Just ahead are Kidzville and Nickelodeon Splat City, two areas designed exclusively for children to enjoy (some attractions can accommodate parents as well). Both areas together feature dozens of attractions for the kiddies, with theming based on Hanna-Barbera cartoon characters. Note: If the day is meant to focus on these areas, when you enter the park in the morning, head left and get right on Delta Flyer and travel to the back of the park—the sky ride disembarks right next to both the kids sections. The park scores high marks for offering a sensational coffee house known as Cup O'Joe right between the two kids sections. It's a gourmet coffee shop, and a great place to relax while the kids are roaming through Kidzville.

Water rides in the park include a flume, a river rapids, and a shoot-the-chute. The park currently opens these rides at approximately 12 noon and closes them at dusk. They are fun, but not entirely essential. If you feel like a splash, though, check the lines during your travels around the park and board them as you please.

As dusk falls, and it gets closer to park closing time, the back half of the park will begin to empty out, and those rides nearest the front will begin to get all the action. Plan to hang back and enjoy the rides in the back of the park as the day comes to an end, as the lines on these will get shorter and shorter toward the end of the day. The area that clears first includes the Psycho Mouse, Drop Zone Stunt Tower, and Grizzly. This low-wait-time area keeps expanding in both directions the closer it gets to closing time, which will just leave more riding time for you and your group.

SANTA CRUZ BEACH BOARDWALK

400 Beach Street
Santa Cruz, California 95060
408-423-5590
www.beachboardwalk.com
Admission: Free Admission to Boardwalk. Pay-one-price wristband, $24.
    Ride tickets priced at 60 cents each, up to $3.60 per individual ride.
Operating Schedule: Open daily Memorial Day to Labor Day, weekends
    and holidays throughout the rest of the year. The park opens at 11 A.M.
    on most operating days, and closes as late as 11 P.M. during the main
    season.

Park History

The Boardwalk has an illustrious history. It began as a resort area with bath houses and pavilions back before the turn of the twentieth century. A casino was added in 1904, which burned down in 1906 and was replaced by an even more elaborate showplace of buildings in 1907, including a new casino, a ballroom, and the boardwalk. The National Historic Landmark Charles I.D. Looff carousel was added in 1911, and in 1924, the Giant Dipper roller coaster, also a National Historic Landmark, was installed at a cost of $50,000 (it costs three times that amount just to paint the ride nowadays). During the twentieth century, the park thrived while many others of its ilk were being replaced by residential structures. The casino was renovated and became the Cocoanut Grove, modern rides were added alongside historic classics, and today, the park is one of the great American amusement park experiences.

Major Attractions

Giant Dipper—National Historic Landmark wooden roller coaster

Carousel—National Historic Landmark 1911 Looff carousel

Cave Train—Dark ride featuring classic and modern displays

Ghost Blasters—Interactive dark ride

Logger's Revenge—Flume ride

Getting There

Take Highway 17 or Highway 1 to Santa Cruz, California, and follow street signs to Santa Cruz Beach. The town is located seventy miles south of San Francisco, California.

Planning to Go

The park is open year round, on weekends only through spring, fall, and winter. It is traditionally closed at the beginning of December. Off-season hours are limited, so check with the park before your visit to verify operating hours.

Unbearable crowds won't be found here, and it will be possible to visit on weekends during the height of the summer without having to spend hours in any lines. The best time to visit to beat any lines whatsoever is spring and fall weekends, but there will be few special events planned during those times, so you might want to plan to visit even during busy summer days.

The park offers discount coupons on its Web site, and also a season pass for only $53 (which is almost the price of a one day Admission at most theme parks). There are also days with limited operation that the wristband price is considerably discounted, and 1907 nights, where pricing is rolled back even more. Check the park's website for info on all special discounted events planned.

You might want to stay in a hotel located within Santa Cruz to enjoy the entire town's offerings for more than one day. Make it a mini-vacation.

Beginning Your Day

The park is located in a charming, Northern California seaside town. If you're up early, explore the town, or enjoy a few hours of sun on the beach (the mornings can be chilly in this part of the country, so don't expect the water to be too warm). Parking for the beach and Boardwalk are located across Beach Street in several lots. They are all conveniently located.

Hardcore ride addicts should plan on purchasing a pay-one-price wristband, which will enable you to ride all the park's rides unlimited for the entire day. An upgrade to the wristband also includes a choice of several of the upcharge attractions in the park. If you're the type that can make do with just a few spins on a ride here and there, opt to purchase ride tickets, valued at $.60 each and good for all rides. These can be purchased either in a sixty ticket strip at a discount, or individually, with rides priced from $1.80 to $3.60.

In the Park

Santa Cruz Beach Boardwalk is a park you should do leisurely; you don't have to run from one ride to another in order to beat crowds and cram enough in to get your money's worth.

The park is long and narrow, with one midway stretching its entire length. The boardwalk that gives the park its name was entirely replaced by concrete, but that doesn't remove its nostalgic atmosphere. There's a lot to do here, and it can all be done totally at your leisure, since no matter what end of the park you start at, or what time of day it is, you'll get it all in, with healthy breaks in between to relax. You'll want to soak up the atmosphere here, not run from ride to ride.

Since this is a park to enjoy at whim, we're just going to take a

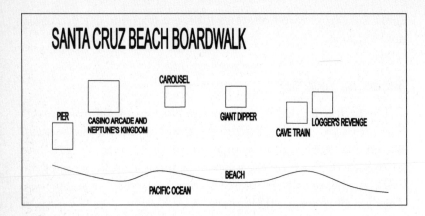

look at the rides and attractions at the park that you won't want to miss.

Giant Dipper is the park's most popular ride, and a National Historic Landmark wooden roller coaster. Built in 1924, it's seventy feet high and about 2,600 feet of twisting, swirling drops and turns. The ride begins with a dive out of the station into a tunnel that snakes its way to the lift hill, where it climbs to the apex before plunging down a sixty-five-foot drop into a fantastic fan turn (horseshoe-shaped turn with no level track). From there, plenty of hills and turns await, with several diving under other portions of structure, creating "headchopper" effects that will make you duck in your seat. The ride is thrilling without being severe, and can be ridden by all. The entrance is located near the middle of the park, in a Victorian style building.

Catch the brass ring on the 1911 Looff Carousel. It's one of the only remaining carousels in the country to offer this classic opportunity to riders on the outside row of the beautiful seventy-three hand-carved horses on the ride (also included are two chariots). The carousel comes complete with its original band organ, constructed in 1894 and still going strong.

The Cave Train, located near the southern end of the park, was built originally in 1961 and was refurbished for a grand opening in

Santa Cruz's beach and boardwalk, with the Landmark Giant Dipper Coaster.
(*Credit: Courtesy of Santa Cruz Beach Boardwalk*)

2000. It's a completely enclosed, underground train ride, featuring dinosaurs and many other stunts and scenery, and has always been a park favorite. The restoration included additional modern stunts and machinery.

Logger's Revenge, the park's flume ride located at the southern end of the boardwalk, is a watery journey fifty-five feet above the midway, ending with a steep splashdown.

Ghost Blasters is an interactive dark ride, featuring the sort of fun usually offered at a shooting gallery combined with a dark ride adventure. Guests on board the vehicles each have their own gun and shoot at the targets inside the ride as they travel through the course, and score points with each successful hit of the target.

Rock and Roll is a spinning circular ride that features swinging cars, and is themed to the 1950s look of hot rods and hot music. Ride this one more for the look and the sound than anything else. Tsunami is a 360-degree looping ride, flipping sixty passengers head over heels both forward and reverse. Hurricane, a small steel coaster, features a tight layout with steep drops and turns, including a helix that is banked at a steep eighty degrees.

For a great view of the park and ocean, try the Skyglider, a ski-lift-style sky ride that spans the boardwalk from one end to the other, and offers a relaxing journey as well as a terrific vantage point from which to scope the location of everything in the park.

Casino Arcade and Neptune's Kingdom are both huge arcades, featuring all the latest video games and some all-time classics. The Kingdom, in the park's former Plunge (swimming pool) building, also offers billiards and two different mini-golf courses. They are both open late, to extend the fun of a day at the Boardwalk even longer.

The Boardwalk also offers a pier, dozens of restaurants and shops, a bowling alley right across the street, weekly concerts, and various other forms of entertainment. And like all seaside boardwalks and amusement areas, it really becomes a magical place at night, when thousands of twinkling, colorful lights blaze into glory and transform the natural beauty into a mystical wonderland.

SIX FLAGS MAGIC MOUNTAIN

26101 Magic Mountain Parkway
Valencia, California 91355
661-255-0100
www.sixflags.com
Admission: $45
Operating Schedule: Open year round. Daily operations late spring through Labor Day, and weekend only through the rest of the year. Park opens at 10 A.M. on most operating days, with closing times varying depending on season.

Park History

When Magic Mountain opened in 1971, it was Southern California's third major theme park, and struggled for a few seasons to find its identity. It found it in a big way by becoming a "white knuckler's" paradise, adding super thrill rides galore. The park's Great American Revolution, installed in 1976, was the world's first 360-degree looping coaster, and Colossus, the huge twin tracked wooden racer, was the world's tallest when it debuted in 1978. The park eventually was purchased by Six Flags Theme Parks, which continued the legacy of making this Southern California's "thrill park" destination. The park is currently tied (with Cedar Point) for having the most roller coasters in the world (a whopping sixteen), and it also boasts the world's tallest coaster, Superman The Escape, a towering 415 feet above the ground.

Major Attractions

X—200-foot-tall steel looping coaster with revolving seats

Viper—One of the tallest standard sit-down coasters on earth

Goliath—Steel non-looping hyper coaster

Colossus—Giant dual-track wooden coaster

Superman The Escape—Steel shuttle coaster / reverse freefall

Riddler's Revenge—Steel looping stand-up coaster

Scream—Steel looping floorless coaster

Getting There

Take I-5 to the Magic Mountain Parkway exit in Valencia, California. If travelling north, make a left turn at the light, or a right turn if heading south, onto Magic Mountain Parkway, and continue to the parking lot toll booths.

Planning to Go

A Six Flags season pass is essential. Plan to purchase one at the first Six Flags park you visit in the season. The pass must be processed at the park you purchase it in. Discounts on day tickets can be found at fast food chains, on food products, etc. Check with the park to see which ones are in effect at the time of your visit. The discount will be greater on weekdays than on weekends.

The park is open year round, but weekends only during non-summer months. Maintenance can force closure of certain rides during the off-season, so if you plan to visit during those months, be prepared to miss a few things. Also keep in mind that although Six Flags stresses that it is a family chain, this park really relies on thrill rides as its mainstay, so if you're a thrill junkie, there'll be plenty more in this park for you to do than at any other park in the state of California.

One last thing: remember that Six Flags tends to stagger ride opening times, so that not everything in the park opens at park-opening time. Unless a particular ride is down for the day due to maintenance, it should open by mid-afternoon. Most of the major rides are not affected by this.

Beginning Your Day

Arrive at the Magic Mountain Parkway early, as parking booths can back up due to a lack of staffing early in the morning (all booths won't be manned). You'll drive right past the main gate and head on down a hill, and around the park to the parking lot, so arriving early won't necessarily guarantee you a spot within a short walking distance. You'll have to walk up a hill to the gate, so try to hop on board a tram, so you won't already be tired of walking before you even enter the park.

Right inside the main gate is the entrance to Hurricane Harbor, the park's water park. Combo tickets can be purchased for both the water park and theme park. You'll never get to do both in one day

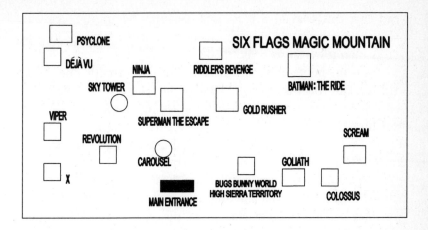

without missing many of the attractions, so bypass a Hurricane Harbor visit and concentrate on the theme park instead.

In the Park

When you enter the park, you'll be in Six Flags Plaza, the park's entry portal. The first thing you'll want to do is check to see if the huge yellow and purple coaster to the left of Six Flags Plaza is up and running with passengers. If it is, head right for it, as the shortest wait for it will be first thing in the morning. This is X, a newfangled thrill machine that features riders sitting two abreast on either side of the track, in vehicles that actually flip 360 degrees forward and reverse during the course of the ride. From a 200-foot height, the passenger trains literally plummet straight down, with riders yanked head first to the ground. The rest of the ride is a blur of spirals, inversions, and twists, and it's unforgettable. Keep your fingers crossed that it's running early in the day when the park opens—it's a prototype, so it tends to shut down frequently. Plus, the loading procedures are quite sluggish; lines of three hours or more have been known to occur.

Hopefully you've tackled X right away (if the line isn't too long, do it again—you won't get on it again for the rest of the day), so head up the midway in Baja Ridge to Samurai Summit. This is the uppermost portion of the park, easily discernable by the 330-foot observation tower at its peak.

This is the home of Superman The Escape, currently one of the world's tallest roller coasters, and one of the fastest. A fifteen passenger vehicle is launched by linear induction motors into a long straight-away, which then becomes a 90-degree vertical climb. At the top, the car simply slows to a hault, and gravity pulls it backwards down the track, back to the station. There's a terrifying and exquisite moment of weightlessness at the top of the tower that always causes butterflies in the stomach and tingles in the spine. The ride features two tracks running side by side, and a car on each track, but often only one side is available, so get to it as early as you can.

While at the top of Samurai Summit, take a whirl on Ninja, the park's fabulous terrain-hugging suspended coaster. The cars swing wildly with each turn, and the track continually heads on down the side of the mountain in unpredictable hills and spirals (a lift hill at the end of the ride carries it back to the station). This is a non-stop, medium thrill experience. If you're doing well on time, take a tour to the top of the world on the park's observation tower, which carries riders in an elevator to a deck nearly 300 feet in the air. The view is breathtaking from the top.

Leave Samurai Summit using the foot path down the back of the mountain into the Movie District section. The giant green steel monster before you is Riddler's Revenge, a stand-up coaster ranked as one of the best of its kind in the world. Because of the restraints found on the ride, loading might take a while, and hopefully you'll arrive at this section of the park early enough to avoid dealing with such a line. Once strapped in, you'll be encountering several loops, corkscrews, twists, and turns along nearly a mile of gnarled track, all while standing up. The ride is very intense and smooth at the same time.

Cross into the Gotham City Backlot section (heading clockwise out of the Movie District), and get on the line to Batman The Ride. This inverted, outside-looping steel coaster with ski-lift-style seating is Six Flags' signature ride (copies exist in all major Six Flags parks). It's a very brief but super intense experience, with five inversion elements taken at lightning pace.

After your flight, stroll into Colossus County Fair, a section with dozens of games, plus two of the signature rides in the park: Colossus, a huge wooden racer, and Goliath, an even bigger steel hyper coaster.

The entrance to Colossus is found by making a hard left out of the Gotham City Backlot section. Unless the park is particularly crowded, only one side of this racing coaster will be operational (although this is often the case even when the park is crowded). Although both sides open will mean significantly shorter lines, you won't be able to know if and when the other track will open. So if only one side is indeed available, grit your teeth and hope that the line isn't too long. This is a very famous roller coaster, having appeared in many films and television shows. At 125 feet tall, it's a huge, massive ride that is surprisingly suitable for many family members.

Leaving Colossus, hang a left, walk under the track for Superman The Escape, and head for the entrance to Goliath right ahead on your left. Goliath is the tallest full-circuit coaster in the park. The ride features a 255-foot drop into a tiny tunnel, and finishes with some of the wildest turns to be found on any roller coaster, anywhere. The very open two-across seating leaves riders feeling vulnerable to the elements and offers an extremely smooth, pleasant but thrilling ride.

It's time to head back to Six Flags Plaza, and catch the second tier of rides in the park. Your journey back to the starting point will bring you through Bugs Bunny World and High Sierra Territory, home to the park's children's areas. If you have children in tow, stop a while in these sections, and let them enjoy themselves—you'll enjoy the rest you get as well.

Back at Six Flags Plaza, you can do one of two things. You can shop for souvenirs in the main gate gift shops, where almost all park merchandise is available, or you can continue riding. A good ride to

Some familiar park residents. (*Credit: Courtesy Six Flags Magic Mountain*)

start off your second round of rides is the park's beautiful antique carousel, built circa 1912 and restored by Magic Mountain in 1971.

Located near the carousel, the Revolution coaster is one of the park's signature rides, debuting in 1976 as the world's first 360-degree looping coaster. Not only is this a thrilling ride, it relies on traditional roller coaster elements like hills, swoops, and turns to deliver the goods, and the single loop mid-course is almost anti-climactic in today's world of multiple inversion giants.

Travelling in a clockwise direction again, head up the hill into Baja Ridge. Unless X has a very short line (it could happen, but probably won't), go directly to Viper, the huge looping coaster just past the entrance to X. This is a seven-inversion, classic looping sit-down coaster, with a 188-foot first drop, three 360-degree loops, a double corkscrew, and a boomerang element. It is still one of the world's largest looping coasters and provides an intense and thrilling ride.

Just past Viper is one of the park's water rides, Roaring Rapids, a river raft ride that was the first of its kind in the West. The seats in the twelve-passenger boats vary as to who gets wet, who gets soaked, and who stays dry, so you never know what's going to happen. This can be a fun experience for the entire family.

If you were one of the Roaring Rapids passengers to get soaked, you might want to take a moment to dry off (in the dry California climate, it won't take long). Head left from the rapids ride and down the hill into Cyclone Bay. This is an area with quaint shops, crafts, and gift items with a seaside village theme. Take a few minutes and browse through the shops. The two main rides here are Psyclone, a wooden coaster that closely resembles the original Coney Island Cyclone in looks and layout but not ride experience (this one is far milder), and Déjà Vu, a huge inverted boomerang shuttle. Neither of these is a must-ride. In fact, Déjà Vu, a prototype design, is quite frequently not operating, so even if you feel you must ride it, you might not be able to. If both rides are operating, and both lines are long, opt for the Psyclone for the shorter wait time, or Déjà Vu for the bigger thrill, but be prepared for Déjà Vu to stop operating during your wait in line—it's been known to do just that.

When you've had your fill with Cyclone Bay, stroll into the Movie District again. Bypass the flume located in this area (a much better one exists further along in your travels), but definitely check out Gold Rusher. This was the park's first roller coaster. It's a mine train that follows the terrain of the mountain it's perched on. While not a great thriller, it's a fun little ride, suitable for the entire family, and you'll be glad you experienced it.

Feel free to hop on any flat rides you encounter along the way in the Movie District or Gotham City Backlot at this time. They are strictly carnival-type rides, so don't expect much from them other than a break from the big thrill rides. You've seen all these before at other parks, with better and longer ride cycles, although probably not with the theming.

The games located in Colossus County Fair are high-priced versions of the standard boardwalk games. Some have much higher levels of difficulty than others, and some are easy to win. Don't get hooked on trying to win the giant Tweety—you could wind up spending more money than it would take to buy one outright. However, this is another great area to slow down and enjoy the atmosphere.

Back in High Sierra Territory, there are a few more spinning rides, typical carnival rides that have been themed, so ride them at your leisure. Also in this section is the park's main water flume, Log Jammer. It hugs the terrain of the mountain, is quite scenic and fun, and climaxes with a terrific drop to the base of the mountain. It's not your typical flume ride.

Once again back in Six Flags Plaza, you may notice a small blue and white steel coaster near the border between the theme park and the water park. This is Flashback, a back and forth zig-zagging coaster that is perhaps the world's worst coaster experience. Not only is it quite boring, but it's rough, slows to a crawl at points, and is repetitive. Thankfully, it is closed most of the time because of its proximity to Hurricane Harbor, so you won't even be tempted to ride it. If you are, you may just deserve what you get. Be warned.

Park food is pricey, as it is in all Six Flags parks. It is recommended that you bring a lunch in a cooler and eat at your car. There are plenty of restaurants near the park where you can enjoy a late dinner, so opt for a snack in the park instead, which will hold you over 'til your late dinner.

As closing time approaches, enjoy Cyclone Bay, the Movie District, or Gotham City Backlot attractions, as they are all located in the back of the park, and the crowds will be thinning out earlier there than in the front. Baja Ridge, with X and Viper, will probably remain packed 'til the bitter end. You can shop at the Six Flags Plaza gift shops as you leave the park, but be warned: there's a souvenir item for almost every major ride in the park, and you'll probably want to take all of them home with you as a remembrance of your visit.

SIX FLAGS MARINE WORLD

2001 Marine World Parkway
Vallejo, California 94589
707-643-6722
www.sixflags.com
Admission: $44
Operating Schedule: Late March through Halloween. Park opens 10 A.M.,
  closing time varies with season.

Park History

This was originally a park known as Marine World/Africa USA, housed in a different location. This animal exhibit park relocated to Vallejo, and began adding major rides when Six Flags signed a management contract with the park. The park now contains one of the best collections of rides, shows, and attractions of any park in the country, with something for everyone.

Major Attractions

Medusa—Steel, looping floorless coaster
Roar—Wooden 1920s-style twister
V2 Vertical Velocity—Suspended linear induction motor launch
  shuttle coaster
Tiger Island—Big cat exhibit and show
Dolphin Harbor—Bottlenose dolphin exhibit and show
Zonga—Steel looping coaster

Getting There

Take I-80 to the Marine World Parkway exit (highway 37) and follow signs to parking lot.

Planning to Go

A Six Flags season pass is essential. Discounts for regular park admission are available through fast food outlets, major supermarket chains, and special promotions. Call the park to determine which are available at your time of visit.

The park is at its best early in the season on weekends, and crowds won't be too much of a problem at this time. Since many guests come here with families in tow to enjoy the animal exhibits, the ride lines can be manageable most of the time.

Beginning Your Day

Get to the park early, as the parking lot is actually a long walk from the main gate (it's located on the other side of a lake from the park). You'll want to park as close to the tramway as possible, so if you do decide to walk, you won't have as far to go. In order to get to the park from the expressway, you'll have to drive a short distance on local streets with traffic lights, and with heavy traffic, this can be a nightmare, so the earlier you arrive to beat the crowds, the better.

Once in the lot, you'll be impressed at how imposing the park looks from that distance. And whether you walk to the main gate or take the tram, you can't but help be blown away by the fact that as you approach the main gate, you are surrounded by three of the main coasters in the park. They're at either side of the entrance, and yet a fourth straddles your path, so you'll have to walk directly under the track.

The first thing you'll need to pick up is a show schedule, as animal shows are a major part of a visit to this park. Plan your day accordingly.

In the Park

Once in the main gate, you'll realize that all the tall roller coasters are right in the front of the park, near the main entrance, but not

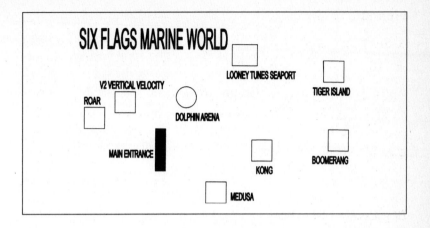

always accessible from that area. The park has a strict height ordinance to follow. 150 feet is the tallest a ride can be in the park, and that is only for rides located near the entrance (it goes down even further as you venture into the park), so all the main coasters had to be built right at the front of the park.

This is a park that has a lot of offerings for everyone. Yes, it has thrill rides, and yes, it has family rides. It also has a terrific selection of animal exhibits and attractions, so you won't be spending your day just riding. Since many of the animal exhibits rely on a schedule, we'll take a tour of the not-to-be-missed rides first, then talk about the animal shows. Their schedule will determine how you spend much of your visit.

Inside the main gate, take a hard right, and then another. This will bring you into a dead-end area with two roller coasters. One, Cobra, is a small family ride consisting of a figure-eight that is actually a lot of fun for everyone. The other, a huge green and purple monster, is Medusa, one of the world's best steel coasters. This 150-foot-tall giant is a floorless coaster, meaning that the passenger vehicles do not contain floors, fronts, or sides, leaving passengers riding on a seat directly attached to wheels. The track layout offers seven inversions, five of which begin the ride in fast succession. The last two are contained in the finale, which is a wild series of left turns that make you feel as if you're being drilled into the ground. Because of the close proximity the ride shares with the nearby community, the track is filled with sand, creating an almost silent journey through the sky (although the screams of the riders aren't all that quiet). Feel free to take several spins on this beauty—it's very smooth and re-rideable.

Leaving this area, turn right and head to Kong, a suspended looping coaster that is good for a spin. This frequently has the longest line in the park because of a single train operation. If the line is too long, only ride it if it's not going to interfere with a show time you have scheduled.

Return to the main entrance plaza area. You passed both a wooden coaster (Roar) on your way into the park, and walked under a steel inverted shuttle right before the main gate. You'll now be heading for those, but don't expect a short walk.

Take the walkway that runs in a straight line next to the main gift shop on the other side of the entrance plaza from where you just came. Continue along this path until you come to the giant arena, and walk left around that. You've just done an about face and are heading back in the general direction of the entrance. Ahead, you'll see your two objectives, Roar and V2. As you reach Roar, to the left is the towering spike of V2. Head for that and the ride's entrance. V2 Vertical Velocity is a linear induction shuttle coaster with one completely vertical 90-degree spike, and, at the other end, a 45-degree spiralling track. When built in 2001, both spikes reached up 90 degrees, but it was then discovered that the forward, spiralling spike was above the strict height ordinance, so for 2002, the ride had to be rebuilt into its present design, making it the only one of its kind in the world. The redesign might also have given V2 an extra notch in the thrills department—the spiral now turns the train through a 360-degree barrel-roll inversion, whereas before, it didn't go upside down at all.

A left turn when leaving V2 will bring you to one of the world's great wooden roller coasters. Roar, designed with spiral drops and sudden direction changes, is an homage to the great twisting mas-

Palm trees and roller coasters abound at Six Flags Marine World. (*Credit: Frank De Santis*)

terpieces that were built in the 1920s. What completely brings this concept home, however, are the ride's trains, which are replicas of an old style vehicle that was prevalent during the 1920s as well. These beautiful, single seat trains hug the turns and snake through their course better than any other wooden coaster trains, increasing the speed, the thrills, and the nostalgia. This is a *great* ride experience.

Throughout the rest of the park, there are many flat rides to be had; most are standard carnival types with heavy theming in some cases, and a few are worth checking out. White Water Safari is a rapids ride, heavily themed with large circular passenger boats travelling through a wet and wild course. Voodoo is a revolving forty-passenger ride that begins with a motion like a demented ferris wheel, but soon flips riders head over heels. Dinosphere TurboRide, an indoor motion simulator in 3-D, features a journey to a volcanic island inhabited by giant reptiles. And of course there's Looney

Tunes Seaport, the children's area located near the shoreline of the park's lake, which offers pint-sized versions of the park's bigger rides.

Half the fun of a visit to Six Flags Marine World is visiting the animal exhibits and seeing the wild life shows. There are plenty to see to fill the entire day even without experiencing any rides, and most are on a schedule, so let's take a look at the must-see's.

Dolphin Harbor is the park's most popular show. It features a selection of playful bottlenose dolphins in an aquatic setting, and it's educational as well as entertaining; Tiger Island features amazing Bengal tigers in a show that proves that all cats don't hate water; The Sea Lion Show, featuring "Jillian's Island," is filled with comic moments as it tells the tale of a survivor who is desperately trying to get off the island. There's also the Birds in Flight Show, and the Wildlife Theatre, featuring "Dr. Wanda de Globe's Wild Life Tails." All are entertaining, and offer insight into the animal world that shares our planet.

Ride lines throughout the park increase a bit in size once the last shows are scheduled, so if you want to get another ride on something, you'd best do it while shows are playing. Otherwise, the rides with the thinnest crowds will probably be Roar and V2, as they are the major rides with the furthest walk times from the main gate. Guests will probably hop on Medusa on their way out, since it's close to the exit.

While food is the standard price and quality for Six Flags, the park doesn't try to keep every dollar you bring in with you by way of merchandise. There is only one major outlet for park souvenirs, located in the main gate plaza area, and they have a limited selection. It's very clear that the park would rather you leave with fond memories (and enough cash to get home) than souvenirs and expensive items you might decide you don't need in the long run.

There *will* be a rush to board trams at the end of the day, so you might want to opt for a casual stroll back to the parking lot. Take your time, because it's a lovely walk that you can enjoy by discussing the fun you had in the park.

Index